# Dead Wrong

## And Other Episodes From a Life in Medicine

## by Thomas H. McConnell, MD

*For Marianne*

# Contents

# Acknowledgments

That these pages are readable owes much to a succession of editors. I first felt the effect of professional editing in the hands of the editorial staff at Lippincott Williams and Wilkins, publisher of two scientific textbooks with my name on the cover. Lonnie Christiansen edited the first one, a textbook of pathology. To say that we clashed is an understatement. Even so, her guidance was invaluable. My second effort, an anatomy and physiology textbook coauthored with Kerry Hull, was edited by Laura Bonazzoli, from whom I learned even more. Barbara Miercort, an accomplished professional writer and friend, edited this manuscript. Anne McConnell Koch edited the hard-copy proof.

✻ ✻ ✻

Cartoons courtesy W. W. West, Jr., MD.  Thanks, Bill.

# In the Beginning

*Rural northeast Texas, about 1944.*

**When did you learn that elephants are big**, that it isn't polite to cut in line, that you can drown in water, that a triangle has three sides, or that we are prisoners on a lonely planet, lost among the stars? With one exception, I can't tell you when I learned any of these things. But I can tell you exactly when I discovered the heavens. It was one of those moments unnoticed by adults but embossed forever into the mind of a child, when Providence washed over me like a tide.

I was six or seven years old. We lived in a little white clapboard house that faced the setting sun. A concrete walk led to the street through the front yard, much of which was trampled into barren submission by the callused bare feet of cavorting boys and girls. On untrod ground sand burs propagated in affirmation of Darwin's maxim of the survival of the fittest.

In the summertime after sunset my father liked to lead us out of the house into the front yard, seeking a breeze as the day cooled into darkness. He and Mother sat on the front porch smoking. He preferred Camels; her brand was Chesterfields. My brother, Jim, and I frolicked in the yard with neighborhood kids, caught lightning bugs in a jar and played hide-and-go-seek and Simon-says. As the light faded and our playmates scampered home in response to shouted calls up and down the street, I liked to lie on my back on the concrete walk and feel the warmth of the departed sun. It offered cozy proof against the encroaching night. I soaked in the hum of cicadas and eavesdropped on my parents as they discussed the war and the events of the day.

There weren't many distractions. Cars rarely came by, I can't recall hearing or seeing an airplane, air pollution was unknown, and a dim streetlight offered the stars little competition. Even so, there was a lot to see as daylight drained away—dragonflies and barn swallows swirled in the air above, and lightning bugs coded their way through the condensing dusk near the ground. But it was the stars that interested me most. As the sky darkened I liked to search for the first star and when I found it I repeated the nursery rhyme Mother taught me:

*"Star light, star bright,*
*First star I see tonight,*
*Wish I may, wish I might,*
*Have the wish I wish tonight."*

Each night I had the same wish—to see the first star the instant it first appeared. But I was never able to catch it. I would survey the sky with all of my concentration, but it was never enough. Try as I might the first star always appeared when I wasn't looking. I would search and find the sky blank, and look again to find it winking. The mystery enthralled me.

One evening well after dark when the stars seemed especially bright my father pointed out the Milky Way and told me how it was made up of many, many stars that were too far away to be seen individually.

"How big are the stars?" I asked him.

"That is a very good question, son," he replied from the steps behind me, out of my view. "They are very big. They look small because they are very far away."

"As big as an elephant?" I asked, thinking of the first really big thing that crossed my mind.

"Much bigger," he answered.

"As big as our house?" I persisted, my eyes full of the tiny lights.

"Oh, yes, son," he said. "The stars are very, very big and very, very far away." I heard him take a deep drag on his cigarette and heave a sigh.

I tried again. "As big as the courthouse?" I said, naming the biggest object I'd ever seen, the red granite courthouse on the square downtown.

He laughed. "Much, much bigger. Son, each one is bigger than the whole world."

In an indelible moment I vested the sky with depth. Forever unfolded before my eyes, and a feeling flooded over me that has not been equaled since. Grasping the limitlessness of the heavens, and charged with new consciousness, I felt plunged into the ocean of space. The world around me receded and I was loosed in the heavens, afloat on a cozy space platform. My head swam and I had a familiar, hollow feeling in the pit of my stomach, the one I got when Mother read Bible stories and told me about heaven and how when I got there I would live forever, and ever, and ever. The world had begun to spin.

It was the beginning of a lifelong romance. A few years later, after I learned about the speed of light, I would stand in the same spot and aim my father's big flashlight at one star and then another, flashing my initials toward them in the Morse code I was learning … *dah … dit dit dit dit … dah dah.* I watched each star like a lover, looking out the beam of light, my neck arched, growing stiff in the evening chill, as I imagined my messages racing through the void. I think of them still.

# Dead Wrong

CHAPTER 1

# A Matter of Honor

**Prologue**

I entered medical school in the fall of 1958.

"**S**on, we don't just let people out of jail because some-one is here to get them. I know it's your mother, but we got rules in this jail," the cop said, leaning over the counter toward me for emphasis.

"Yes, sir," I said, hoping that my crisp white shirt, rep tie, dark suit, buzz haircut, good English, and earnest, submissive attitude would do the trick, but his stern look didn't offer much promise.

It was Sunday and I'd been at the Dallas city jail much of the morning, the same jail where a few years later Jack Ruby would slay Lee Harvey Oswald. I had slowly worked my way up the chain of authority, trying to get my sweet, troubled mother out of jail because the night before she had slammed into a police car that was running at full bore, lights flashing, siren's wailing. Never mind that she had the green, she should have yielded, but she didn't. These things happen if you are drunk, and she was.

For a moment I considered explaining what was at stake. I needed to get her out, not just for her sake, but for mine, too—I was a sophomore medical student in the middle of a 48 hour weekend drill, collecting my own urine for a biochemistry lab experiment. My bladder was getting full, and I had to get back home to the big jug in the bathroom. Letting my precious load go down the toilet would be the end of my experiment. And I didn't know what to expect if I didn't turn in the expected paper.

But it was too much to explain. On my side of the counter was a scrum of surly humanity, each sure to have some sad, desperate story. Mine, while novel, surely ranked low on the sympathy scale. So, I just let it go with, "Yes, sir," and blankly stared back at the cop.

He gave me a hard look and after a pause took the papers and stuck his head in the office door behind the counter. A few words were exchanged and the cop stood aside for a man in a suit and tie who came to the door. He examined the papers and gave me his version of a long, hard look. "Let the boy have his mother," he said.

But it proved to be too late. By the time the paper-work was finished and she came meekly through the door I'd already sent my experiment down the toilet.

Monday morning in biochemistry lab everyone else bustled about in their long white coats, a cloak of inferior status in the strict symbolism that ruled the academic empire. So there I stood, not knowing what to do. I explained my problem to the student work-ing next to me. I'd met Eddie Sankary on account of his wife, Lynny, who worked as a clerk in the library. I'd made of a fool of myself by making a prissy com-plaint that she talked too much and too loudly for me to study. In spite of my boorish behavior we be-came friends, so it was natural for me to ask him what I should do about my lack of a specimen. He volun-teered to let me work on his specimen; we'd turn it in as a joint project, which we did.

I thought nothing more about it until a week later when I was summoned to the biochemistry office. I was ushered into the presence of a junior professor. Many of us had us had taken a dislike to him because of the air of officious self-importance that clung to him tighter than his perfectly starched and creased white laboratory coats. It was our theory that he didn't like medical students because he was only a PhD and we were going to be MDs.

"I have here the results of your laboratory experi-ment," he said. "Is this the result of your work?"

"Yes, sir," I said, puzzled.

With a flourish he put another paper under my nose. I could see Eddie's name at the top of the paper. "Your results are exactly the same as Mr. Sankary's," he said. "What do you have to say about that?" he said, sitting back with a satisfied little smile.

I felt relieved for a moment. The explanation was simple and compelling. Neither Eddie nor I had tried to hide anything. "Well, sir, it's not exactly mine alone. You see, I . . ."

"So this is not solely your own work, is it?" he interrupted.

"No, sir," I confessed and laid out the details of my trip to the jail and how I had to let my specimen go down the drain in a jail urinal. I should have saved my breath.

"You know what the honor code says about only submitting work you have done yourself, not someone else's," he said, stabbing his finger at the honor code pledge posted at the bottom of the page beneath my signature. "Yes, sir, but . . ." He stood up, ending the interview before I could complete the sentence, and shuffled the incriminating evidence back into a manila folder.

My heart sank. I thought I was going to faint. I knew something about honor codes. I had spent three years at Rice University, which had a famously strict one. All of us at Rice enjoyed the freedom it brought— self-timed take-home tests, no nosy proctors hovering about during exams, and so on. But the other side of the coin was that Rice Honor Council hearings were famously occult and students found guilty suddenly stopped showing up around campus as if liquidated by a secret police. And the code covered all manner of conduct, not just cheating and other academic crimes. During my time there several students were summarily dismissed for bringing a six-pack of beer onto campus in violation of a stern No Alcohol policy and violated the Honor Code by lying about it.

"But, sir," I said, "what else could I do?"

"Well," he said, dismissing my question, "I'm referring both of you to the Honor Council. You'll hear from them soon." He didn't say, "Gotcha!" But he might as well have.

It took a couple of weeks for the Honor Council to convene. In the meantime I was a nervous wreck. Eddie and I testified separately to a council composed of students, two from each class, including two in our class, neither of whom seemed to sense the gravity of the occasion. Dr. Gotcha and several senior professors were also present. I had never been so fearful.

I told my tale, Eddie told his, and we sat outside while our fate was debated. Poor Eddie, all he did was offer to help me out of a jam and here he was, snared in a mess. Finally, the chairman, a senior student, came out and told us we were not to be disciplined, and suggested that if anything like this came up again we should tell the professors in advance. For an instant I was flooded with relief. Then it dawned on me that this sensible advice could have been given to us by Dr. Gotcha.

## Epilogue

Dr. Gotcha had an undistinguished career, never making it to full professor. Eddie became a successful anesthesiologist. I still count him and Lynny among the dearest of friends. He is as generous of spirit now as then, and Lynny still talks as much and as loudly as ever.

# CHAPTER 2

# Dead Wrong

**Prologue**

In 1960, three years before Parkland Hospital was catapulted into world history with the assassination of John F. Kennedy, I was roaming the halls as a junior medical student getting my first taste of patient care.

My first two years had been in the squat medical school classrooms and labs in the shadow of Parkland's hulking tower. The third year, however, marked the beginning of two precious years in Parkland's wards and clinics learning internal medicine, obstetrics, pediatrics, and surgery. Most of our patients were indigent. Private patients wanted air conditioning and private rooms, neither of which Parkland offered.

Care was delivered by a team. Leading each team was a professor, who bore final responsibility. Next in line was a resident, a specialist-in-training, in this instance one learning internal medicine. The resident made most of the important decisions. Then there was an intern, someone who had graduated from medical school the previous year, who supervised bedside care, and monitored patient progress. The lowest lump in this pile was the medical student, me. My job was to start IVs, draw blood, fetch charts, track down missing lab results and x-rays, collect urine and other specimens, and do whatever other "scut work" was required.

"Miss Quench" was one of my first patients. I was 23 years old.


She had curly red hair, freckles and a pleasant, round face, but from the beginning she was a trial.

First, she smelled to high heaven. Second, she was demanding, insolent, ungrateful, and combative. Before her stay ended I was exasperated near to screaming and filled with dread at having to visit her several times each day. I had no greater wish than that she would somehow get off of 6-South, out of Parkland, and out of my life.

But she had good reason to be there. She had appeared in the Parkland emergency room complaining of chest pain. Most such patients were older men with coronary artery disease. But she was a woman in her mid-thirties, not the type to have clogged coronary arteries. On the other hand, she was short, very fat, and she had diabetes and high blood pressure, a dangerous combination that frequently led to heart attacks.

Records indicated numerous previous visits to the emergency room. Typically she had shown up loopy from out of control diabetes, blood pressure raging. Her chart was thick with exasperated notes about bad attitude and poor compliance—she didn't keep appointments and didn't take her medicine. Most of the time she languished for hours, IVs dripping, while insulin and other medicines slowly coaxed her systems back into balance. But this time the emergency room resident couldn't exclude the possibility of heart disease, so despite her youth and sex he put her in a bed on 6-South.

As bad as things were for her, they were good for me; too good, perhaps. I was well on my way to becoming a doctor, and I stood near the top of a class filled with high school valedictorians and *cum laude* graduates from major universities. My academic performance puzzled and dazzled me because it was coming so easily. I'd had a mediocre high school record and had struggled the first year and a half in college, until my father's death, merciful for him and for me, freed me from worry. Good grades and good fortune plopped into my lap like fruit falling from a tropical tree. I felt as though I were a beneficiary as the Universe worked out its purposes. It was heady stuff. I studied, but it was fun, not a chore. I read voraciously—novels, biography, history, newspapers, magazines, you name it. I even had time for a bit of social life, though my financial means were limited. Prestige and new vistas beckoned. Especially intoxicating was the new power I was discovering: license to invade bodies and probe minds, to ask questions not allowed in any other context, and to command others in the name of an altruistic cause. On the last point, however, medical students labored in a vale of shadows, but I could see the sunny higher ground where white-coated authoritarians experienced immediate compliance with their orders.

The drill for newly admitted patients called for me to do a thorough physical and extensive history, never mind that residents and interns had done a focused history, physical exam, lab tests and x-rays in the middle of the night. It was all there for me to read and done better than I could ever hope to do.

Nevertheless, in observance of expected ritual, I asked her a zillion questions from a standard form—"Miss Quench, has anyone in your family had hemorrhoids?"—and poked around in anatomy that had no relevance to the problem at hand—"Miss Quench, I'm going to do a rectal exam to be sure you don't have a cancer in there."

This nonsense did not sit well with her. It was clear that she'd seen enough of Parkland to know where the power lay, and it was not with me. I dutifully asked irrelevant questions.

"Miss Quench, do you ever have headaches?"

"You give me a headache."

"Miss Quench, has anyone in your family ever had colon cancer?"

Silence. She stared at the ceiling.

Her disrespect was palpable. My inclination was to quit. I could probably skip filling out the form on her and no one would care.

But I was on an academic roll and didn't want to break my momentum. I slogged on.

"Miss Quench, tell me about your chest pain."

Animated for the first time, she levered up on an elbow and spoke directly to me.

"It's like a band going around my chest," she said, using her fingers to draw out an imaginary band a few inches wide. She was quite precise.

"It starts here, goes around this side," she said, pointing under her right arm, "and around my back to here," she added, pointing under her left arm, "and back to here," she concluded, pointing to the middle of her chest.

"I have another band going around my stomach," she added, using her fingers the same way.

I had dutifully read about heart pain, and this was not the way it was supposed to be. It should have been dull, diffuse, and difficult to describe—an unpleasant sensation, not exactly pain, but more like a strong fist pushing in on the breast bone. Sometimes it extended to the left neck, jaw or arm.

"None of that," she said with finality and returned to the bands of pain.  It was like she was describing barrel hoops.

Violating technique, I asked leading questions.

"Is the pain sharp or dull?

No answer.

"Does the pain cause a feeling of pressure in your chest?"

Silence.

"What . . ." I began another question.

"Will you leave me alone!" she shouted.  "I've told every one of you what's wrong with me.  Why don't you just give me some medicine to make it go away?"

With as much dignity as I could muster, I closed the chart and walked out, angry and humiliated.  I wrote in the chart what she'd told me even though I knew it was nonsense.

This was my first encounter with the problem of pain. The ability of patients to describe pain is necessarily subjective and more dependent on intelligence and linguistic skill than any other aspect of patient complaints.  Pain is a singular personal experience, so difficult to communicate that it is akin to trying to describe color to a person blind from birth. The average patient, let alone someone like "Miss Quench," is poor at describing pain.  Maybe her pain really occurred as bands around her chest and belly, or maybe if she had better control of language and better self-knowledge, she might have described the pain in a way that would have convinced us that she had heart pain. But she didn't. There is no solution to the problem. Science will never get into someone's mind to determine the "true" nature of pain.

Later in the day she was the subject of much discussion among our team, but it was too early to come to any conclusions other than the strange way she described her pain, how rude she was and how awful she smelled.

The next morning as I was about to turn into her room, I heard a loud argument between her and another woman.

"I'm telling you, it's not working. You have to find some place else to live," the new voice said.

"You can't do that! I've paid my rent!" my patient shouted.

"I don't care. You're not coming back."

"Go to hell. Parkland is a lot cleaner than that filthy hole you call a room. You'll never find anyone else stupid enough to pay the rent!"

Insults flew and her visitor, a rail-thin, middle-aged black woman, stormed out of the room. I decided there were other things I needed to do.

The next day I tried again. My goal was to ask more clever questions to see if I could get an answer to the riddle of the peculiar bands of pain. I would get to the bottom of the mystery by persistence, if nothing else. But she stuck with her story about the bands of pain.

Her reputation among the staff had spread. Nobody could bear to deal with her, even after an aide had given her a bath that eliminated the smell.

Nobody believed her peculiar tale about the bands of pain. It sounded contrived. The blood tests, electrocardiogram and other tests were inconclusive. The idea began to build that she was making it all up. At evening rounds the collective judgment was to send her home. We couldn't find evidence of heart disease; we needed the bed; and she was likely malingering, probably to avoid an unpleasant home environment. But just to be complete, we asked for a psychiatric consult to see what the shrinks thought.

The next morning a psychiatry resident came for a visit and left a useless note about personality disorder and situational stress. Afterward, it was my chore to tell her we were sending her home.

'Miss Quench, we are going to discharge you this afternoon. You need to call someone to meet you on the curb," I sad.

"Y'all are crazy," she fumed. "I've been here nearly a week and you haven't done a damned thing for me. I'm still having these pains. I'm not calling anybody."

Not knowing what to do, I passed the problem off to the resident.

"That woman may be the end of me!" he said, and disappeared down the hall toward her room.

In a few minutes he came back, madder than ever.

"Now we're going to have to get social services involved. She says she doesn't have a place to live and nobody to call. We'll never get that damned woman out of that bed. She likes it here."

It took Social Services a few days to find a place and it fell to me to give her the bad news that she had to leave. Dreading every step, I marched to her room.

"Miss Quench you must get dressed to go home," I said with all the authority I could muster.

"I don't have a home. You know that," she said. "Are you throwing me out on the curb?"

Then, to my astonishment, she sat up in bed and slid her feet to the floor. She looked at me blankly for an instant, her gown and hair a mess.

"I'm having the pain again," she said.

That's it, I thought. She knows the system. She is going to manipulate us into keeping her here.

In a final act of desperation she threw herself on the floor.

As calmly as I could manage, I said, "Get up. This charade is over. You must go home."

She stayed on the floor, making little movements.

"Get up!" I said. "We've had enough of your nonsense."

She would not get up. I went closer and poked my toe into her ribs.

"Get up!" I said again. No response.

She was turning blue. I bent close and pried open her eyes: they were rolled back. Foam bubbled through her lips with a gurgle. I felt her neck for a pulse: nothing. I called for the crash cart.

In the ensuing pandemonium I faded to the periphery, thankful that no one had seen me poke her with my toe. Never had I felt such shame. It was not the red-faced shame of embarrassment, which suffices for the public glare of social faux pas, bounced checks and speeding tickets, but a cold, soul-blanching darkness.

After the bedlam and failed resuscitation, to which I was a dazed spectator, I retreated to the hospital library and sat for a long time, pretending to read a textbook and rebuking myself. All I could do was rerun the loop of our final interaction, which always ended with a still-frame: my toe in her ribs. I tried rationalization. Everyone else had failed to make the correct diagnosis, too, but it brought no solace. None of them had been angry with her and poked her with a toe. Nothing could explain it away. All I could think of was how utterly I had dehumanized her. I had compounded scientific failure with indifference to the human condition, out of which springs all manner of evil, from torture to terrorism.

The next morning I went to the morgue to watch her autopsy. She proved to have severe coronary heart disease and evidence of old and fresh heart attacks.

**Epilogue**

In the ensuing years I've revisited this episode many times, trying to understand how it came to be and how it might have played out in another way. More humility would have helped me. She was fault-less. I was of a mind, without realizing so, that I was right and could not be wrong. In retrospect it seems scripted. I was myself, she was herself, and that was the problem.

If her hospitalization occurred today it is a near certainty that blood tests now available would have produced clear evidence of heart disease and her odd description of pain would merit nothing more than casual interest. However, as good as today's tech-nology is, it is not so good that it can save us from ourselves. In one way or another this scene from long ago is replayed many times each day in modern medicine.

CHAPTER 3

# Psycho-therapy

**Prologue**

   "Miss Quench" aside, I enjoyed patient contact so much that duties and studies seemed more entertainment than work. The thrill energized me, and I cast around for outside work that involved patient contact. One opportunity looked especially appealing, a job as an "extern" at a private psychiatric hospital.

   "You'll love this job," one of the previous externs told me. "They leave most of the night and weekend exams and calls to us. The psychiatrists don't want to be bothered, and it's not like the patients are really sick, they're just crazy. And they're locked up. So, how much trouble can they be? How much harm can you do? When in doubt I just give 'em a big shot of Thorazine," he added, referring to a new antipsychotic drug. "It knocks 'em down until morning when the real doctors show up."

So, on the strength of this dubious endorsement, I signed up to work my final two years of medical school as a paid extern at Timberlawn Psychiatric Hospital, a prestigious private institution where I was one of a team of three medical students who shared call doing after-hours admission interviews and physical exams. During the summer, when school was not in session, I worked daytime making rounds, attending staff meetings, and doing physical exams and medical histories on new admissions.

A s a budding physician-to-be I especially relished the evening hours at Timberlawn. I was the go-to guy if the nursing staff needed help and didn't want to bother the psychiatrist on call. In those two years I saw a textbook's worth of interesting patients, and came to admire psychiatrists. They seemed sage, caring, and majestically above the foibles that roiled the lives of their patients.

I thought regularly about what it might be like to be a psychiatrist. Human behavior interested me and I could be right in the middle of it as a psychiatrist. But there were many other choices. I liked pathology, too. I had made good grades in pathology the previous year. I liked the idea of specimens and the cool, detached rhythms of the laboratory. Pathology or psychiatry?

I was weighing the choice when I began to notice Madelyn. She was a long term inpatient with severe schizophrenia whose big monthly bills were supported by a trust fund. She was completely out of touch with reality, alternately muttering gibberish and talking to unseen friends and tormentors, all the while twisting her face and body into strange shapes. In my two year term I detected not one iota of improvement.

I was a senior medical student in my last year at Timberlawn and still debating the pathology vs. psychiatry choice when Madelyn and a psychoanalyst strolled by hand-in-hand on a walk around the grounds.

"Wooahwu, no Billy. Not! Shmooroyah, uh, gromany. No! No!," Madelyn spluttered and stamped her foot.

"Yes," the analyst said. "Hmm, hmm. Go ahead."

"What the hell," I said to myself. "This is crazy." Psychiatry seemed hopeless.

To be fair, this was in the days before a wave of psychoactive drugs emptied mental hospitals, and ultimately bankrupted Timberlawn. Talking and a few drugs, however, were not the only therapies available. Electric shock and insulin coma were popular.

The former induced epileptic-like seizures by loosing a surge of voltage through the brain. The latter involved injecting a horse-size slug of insulin to drive blood glucose down far enough to induce coma, during which a seizure, if one occurred, was a bonus. The seizures and coma were said to be good for relieving paranoia and depression. Both were wildly beyond anything I had imagined about psychiatric treatment.

As a new extern I had inquired about their scientific basis. "It works . . . some of the time" and "It's about all we have" captures the gist of it.

In both instances patients were amnesiac after treatment. We joked that they were improved because they couldn't remember who they were paranoid about, why they were depressed, or what we had done to them.

For electric shock treatment patients were led into a small windowless room that looked less like a place of healing than an execution chamber where a somber clutch of doctors, nurses and aides waited beside a white-sheeted gurney, big leather straps dangling. As the psychiatrist squeezed the patient's temples between the paddles I imagined him as Dr. Frankenstein. He stepped on the switch connected to a big black box studded with dials, lights, and switches. In a stroke the patient was galvanized by body-wrenching bucks and leaps as current coursed through tender brain cells, whose tiny native electrical currents were overwhelmed by a tsunami of electrons racing from one paddle to the other.

A few patients came willingly, meekly stretched themselves out for our ministrations, and were dispatched straight into oblivion without ceremony. The reluctant were coaxed by their psychiatrist, a trusted advisor and confidante, who seemed to betray the bond psychiatry purported to be at the core of the therapist-patient relationship. But no matter, the deal was going to go down because those who resisted were overpowered, forcibly injected with a sedative, then anesthetized and zapped. It was my job to insert between the patient's jaws a wooden tongue depressor tightly wrapped in cotton cloth, the better to prevent them from chewing their tongue into hamburger. Approaching a patient, final advice from the psychiatrist was "Keep your fingers out of the way."

Inducing insulin coma was equally straightforward but was deployed en masse to an entire wing. First, we injected patients with a jumbo dose of insulin. Before their blood glucose could fall very far we wrapped them, mummy-like, in a sheet and buckled them down with heavy leather straps to keep them from vaulting out of bed if they had a seizure. Afterward we watched as they sank into coma, zombies who only lightly disturbed the eerie silence of the halls with a foam of sighs, burbles, and snores.

It was my job to bring patients out of coma by injecting them intravenously with a jumbo syringe full of glucose.

One especially memorable patient was a paranoid schizophrenic I had been following for several weeks since her admission to the lock-up ward, a domicile reserved for "the craziest of the crazed," as we were fond of saying. Some paranoids are furtive and keep their delusions to themselves. This woman, however, was loud and combative. Radio waves were reading her mind; the staff was engaged in a plot to drain her bank account, a not so delusional thought; and voices no one else could hear were tormenting her unmercifully. But this behavior had abated somewhat, and she had been "promoted" onto the insulin ward.

I loosened her restraints, unwrapped the sweat-soaked sheet to free her arms, found a vein and injected glucose to relight the fires of consciousness. It was always a touchy task because women's veins are usually smaller and less visible than men's and the glucose solution was syrupy, which required a very large needle. Sometimes the needle came out of the vein or was incorrectly inserted in the first place. When this happened the patient could come half way out of coma into a never-never land. We ushered them back into the light with a big glass of super sweetened orange juice.

I goofed up the injection and she didn't wake up fully. I lifted her up to a sitting position on the side of the bed. She looked around uncertainly.

"Mrs. Krankle," I said in my most soothing tone, "you'll feel so much better if you'll have some orange juice."

I held the glass out to her. She took it and looked at me doubtfully.

"I don't know," she said, studying the glass, suspicion written in her frown.

"It's okay," I said. "It's just orange juice. I made it just for you."

She looked up at me.

Suppressed paranoia, molten hot, bubbled up from the depths of her psyche and spewed from her lips.

"You sonofabitch," she said and threw the juice into my eyes.

It stung like hell. She grabbed the ends of my necktie and with surprising strength cinched it tight around my throat. I croaked a call for help and was rescued by a squad of nurses and aides.

She was un-promoted back to the lockup ward. I switched to clip-on ties.

As much as I liked Timberlawn, I couldn't get by on what they were paying me, so I continued with a couple of other jobs. Occasionally, I worked in a night as private duty nurse at Children's Hospital, and once a week or so I did admission examinations at a small clinic-hospital. It was a strain, especially when my medical student schedule put me on duty every third night at Parkland Hospital.

The upshot was that on a particular evening I found myself being on call or at work for a seventeenth consecutive night, this time at Timberlawn. After the drive across town from Parkland, I went straight to bed.

When the phone rang, I might as well have been in an insulin-induced haze.

"Doctor McConnell," the voice said, flattering me. I was no doctor, yet. "This is nurse Midge on Unit D. I'm calling about Miss Spacey. She's has had a seizure.

"Uh, hmm."

"You admitted her last night. Remember, she has a history of Miltown abuse," she said, referring to a new tranquilizer that I knew could cause seizures upon sudden withdrawal.

"Uhm, okay."

"What shall I do?" she asked.

"Well, uhm, just give her a couple of Miltown pills."

"Doctor McConnell, she's too out of it to cooperate and she's been vomiting. I'll never get her to swallow them." This was no surprise. I knew that after a seizure patients were usually drowsy, confused, and nauseous. I should have known without a reminder, but my brain wasn't working very well.

"Hmm. Okay. Er, uh, uh, hmm, just give it to her by injection. That ought to do the trick."

"Doctor McConnell, Miltown is not available in injectable form."

"Just a minute; uh, just let me think," I groaned. I put the phone on the pillow and dozed for a moment before some sound from the receiver brought me back.

Jesus! I knew I should get out of bed and go over there, but I was so drugged by fatigue that I couldn't think straight. To get out of bed seemed impossible. My primary aim became to think of something, anything, that would satisfy the nurse so I could go back to sleep.

"Uh, do they make it as a rectal suppository?" I asked.

"No, sir; tablets are all I have."

I thought for a moment about just telling her to forget it, but the threat of repeated or prolonged and perhaps fatal seizures was not a risk I was willing to take.

There is a saying among doctors that desperate situations call for desperate measures. This was such a moment. I invented a therapy: the tranquilizer enema.

"We're going to have to get it into her rectally," I said. "Make up a warm saline solution and crush four pills. Dissolve them in as little fluid as you can. We don't want her passing them into the toilet. Push the tube as high as you can," I continued, as if I'd done it a dozen times.

I expected the nurse to object, but she didn't. I went back to sleep and the phone didn't interrupt again.

The next morning I awoke with a start. I couldn't recall exactly what had happened. I don't ordinarily eat breakfast, but I opted to go to the cafeteria for coffee and a doughnut before driving across town to the medical school. I wanted to nose around to see what had gone on. Maybe I could engineer a discreet inquiry of the nursing supervisor about the shift report. As luck would have it, the supervisor was in the break room chatting with several other nurses.

They stopped talking when I entered the room.

"Good morning, Doctor McConnell," the supervisor said.

It was common courtesy for externs to be glorified by use of "Doctor"—we loved it—but this time it didn't sound quite right. Did I catch a hint of sarcasm? Paranoia is not confined to schizophrenics. Were they gossiping about me, the idiot extern who ordered the sleeping pill enema? I couldn't bring myself to be direct about it.

"So, ladies, I trust nobody escaped last night," I said, hoping to prod one of them to comment about goings on from the late shift.

"Oh, no sir, just the usual oddities," one of them said. Was a tranquilizer enema an oddity?

I hesitated for a moment, waiting for them to bring up the topic. They didn't, which compounded my fear that they had been talking about me.

"Well, I'll see you later," I said, ending the awkward silence, and headed for Unit D.

After being buzzed in through the security door, I plopped into a chair at the nursing station and did my best imitation of a psychiatrist checking the charts. First, I made a diversionary move and looked at several other charts before picking up the enema patient's chart. With anticipation as great as I felt opening a final exam, I flipped through the pages until I got to the nurses notes. There it was: the sleeping pill enema episode described briefly and with matter-of-fact detachment. Hourly follow-up notes revealed the patient slept quietly the remainder of the night and had no more seizures.

It was the first and last therapeutic enema of my career.

## Epilogue

Poor Madelyn was still there when I graduated from medical school and left Timberlawn. That someone so disturbed was being offered "talk therapy" reflect how little psychiatry had to offer many patients in those days.

Much the same is true for insulin coma therapy. It was in decline even as we used it wholesale. It was not supported by good science, and disappeared altogether shortly after my term at Timberlawn. Thinking back on it gives me chills. It was unscientific and inhumane. It's a wonder we didn't kill someone or render them brain-dead.

Electric shock therapy, however, survives. Usage declined dramatically, but recent years have seen an increased acceptance as a safe, effective and economical tool for the treatment of some mental illnesses. It is offered only to consenting patients after other modes of treatment have proven ineffective.

Freshmen were frazzled by anatomy and physiology.

Sophomores couldn't read or write fast
enough to keep up.

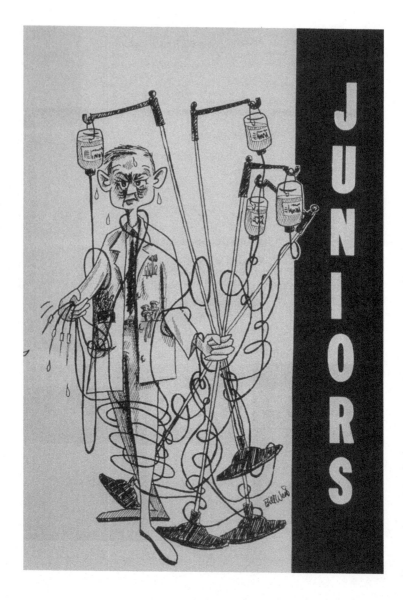

Juniors started a lot of IVs.

Seniors did some minor surgery.

CHAPTER 4

# A Death in Jackson

**Prologue**

   Two years later, from the summer of 1962 to the summer of 1963, I was an intern at the University of Mississippi Hospital in Jackson.

**Y**ou've ruined the specimen again!" the lab tech said, clearly irritated by my ineptness. "It's hemolyzed, just like the first one," she continued, referring to destruction of red blood cells in the tube of blood I'd collected and sent to the lab. I was on the phone and couldn't see her expression, but there was no mistaking the message. She didn't have to say "you idiot," it wasn't necessary. I was just another intern taxing her patience with poor specimens obtained by clumsy stabs at veins.

Thomas H. McConnell, MD

This was not what I wanted to hear. I was the emergency room intern, it was late, and I was alone and desperate. My patient was in deep trouble, and I had no idea what was wrong. I needed the results of her lab tests in the worst way.

I had the other basics. She was a desperately ill young black woman: her general appearance (no evidence of trauma), she was not paralyzed (she was thrashing about), her mental state (delirious, semicomatose), her blood pressure (barely detectable), heart rate (very high), and respiratory rate (rapid). But all of that goes only so far. I needed lab information, I needed it quickly, and I couldn't get it despite having collected two specimens.

Knowing something about the number and type of red and white blood cells was critical for me to sort out what was going on. After ruining the first specimen, I'd taken special care collecting the second one. Her veins were hard to find, collapsed along with her blood pressure, so for my second attempt I chose an especially large syringe and needle—one that would be welcome in the large animal practice of a veterinarian—and jabbed it into her groin, aiming for the big vein that carries blood back to the heart from her right leg. It was a "clean stick," as we said, and I easily sucked out a big specimen, enough to fill several lab tubes. Triumphs of any kind are difficult in medicine, especially in an emergency room, but this was a minor triumph and I felt energized by the experience.

Getting good blood specimens was something I'd excelled at as a medical student, so much so that other students having trouble would call for my assistance. Now, here I was, an intern, a few months out of medical school, having collected hundreds of specimens in my budding medical career, and I had a lab tech telling me the second specimen was bad, too. Something was not right.

"Hold on," I shouted into the phone, "I'll be right there in … ." She hung up in my ear.

I took the stairs two at a stride and found the lab tech, who thrust the tubes toward me for inspection. "See, I told you so. They're both completely hemolyzed," she said, making no effort to disguise her satisfaction at demonstrating proof of my stumblebum status.

Sure enough, she was right. The blood in both tubes had a red, glassy transparency akin to strawberry Kool Aid, an astonishing sight that indicated that all of the red cells, not just some of them, had been destroyed—that is, hemolyzed. I'd seen hemolyzed blood before—it is the first step in doing a common lab test. Ordinarily blood is red, but opaque: you can't see through it because the millions of red cells in every drop blot out transmitted light. And I'd seen plenty of ruined specimens as a medical student, but even the most severely mishandled specimens never ruin *all* of the red cells.

"Let's take a look at a blood smear," I said.

She gave me a skeptical, self-satisfied look, the type that seasoned professionals give to bench warmers. She was a seasoned lab tech. I was an intern. What did I know—the last time I had looked through a microscope was my second year in medical school. Nevertheless, she prepared a smear, and I slid it under the microscope. What I saw I count as one of the most remarkable sights in a long career spent looking at things through a microscope: there were no red cells in her blood. Well, there were a few, but mainly they were fragments of broken cells. The white cells looked okay.

An idea was beginning to form. Some disease was destroying her red cells. By definition, then, she had a hemolytic anemia—"hemolytic" for red cell destruction; "anemia" for too few red cells. I'd studied hemolytic anemias in medical school and I'd even seen a minor case in my junior year. But this was colossal red blood cell destruction.

I asked the tech to do two lab tests on what I had come to believe were valid specimens. First, I asked for a hematocrit measurement, a simple test that measures the percent of blood volume occupied by red blood cells (the remaining fraction is liquid plasma). Normally, the hematocrit (the red cell percent) is about 40% of blood volume and the liquid about 60%. My patient's hematocrit was 1%. It seemed impossible that life could be sustained in such circumstances. Second, I asked for a hemoglobin measurement. Hemoglobin is the oxygen-carrying molecule in red blood cells—a red blood cell is really nothing but a tiny package of hemoglobin. A normal result is about 15 (grams per 100 cubic centimeters of whole blood). My patient's was 9, not terribly low. I had seen anemic patients with lower hemoglobin. The inescapable conclusion was that most of this patient's hemoglobin had escaped from her red cells because something was destroying them, spilling their hemoglobin into the liquid part of blood. My patient was living off of the oxygen carried by hemoglobin in her plasma, a very, very bad set of circumstances for too many reasons to explain here. It was not something I could have imagined.

On my way back to the emergency room I sprinted through the blood bank and ordered two units of blood for transfusion, declaring that I had an extreme emergency on my hands and did not have time for the usual lab tests. Not used to hearing such from an intern, they balked. I told them I didn't have time to argue, that life and death were at stake and they would have to live with the consequences if they didn't do as I said.

While waiting for the blood to arrive, I reviewed what I knew. First, at least for a while, I was on my own. The biggest, busiest and best-staffed ER was the one at another hospital across town. My hospital was new and the emergency room was not very busy. The late night shift was a single intern (me) and a seasoned nurse. A general surgery resident and an internal medicine resident were loose somewhere on the floors above, but it always took a while for them to show up. Most didn't like to come to the emergency room because it usually meant a nettlesome problem or, in their view, a waste of time helping stupid interns. Even more reluctant were chest and neurosurgeons, and the like, who took emergency call duty from home. There they lounged before their black and white TVs watching the National Guard camped out at "Ole Miss" and endless interviews with angry white Mississippians denouncing the invasion of their glorious state by civil rights busybodies, most of whom spoke with strange accents.

I also knew that my patient was a young, adult black woman brought to the emergency room by persons unknown who left quickly without providing much more than the patient's name, age and an address in rural Mississippi. The nurse had tried to start an intravenous drip to keep a vein available but had failed because she couldn't find a good vein. She had managed, however, to insert a catheter into the woman's bladder. The tube ran to a bag hanging on the gurney, but only a tiny amount of ominously black urine had accumulated.

I took stock. The lab information, meager as it was, clarified things mightily. Something was destroying her red bloods cells at a phenomenal rate, and I had to figure out what it was and do something about it. I asked the nurse to page the internal medicine and OB-Gyn residents taking emergency call.

The two pints of blood arrived, but I had no more luck than the nurse in finding an easy vein, they were collapsed due to low blood pressure, but I got an IV running by going back into the big vein in her groin. When the blood came I piggy-backed it onto the IV and squeezed the bags, forcing the blood in. The result was dramatic. Blood pressure rose, heart rate slowed, she awoke from the coma, and I was able to secure cooperation for a vaginal exam and ask her some questions.

There are hundreds of causes of red cell destruction apart from poor specimen collection technique. Most are relatively easy to understand. For example, sometimes a mechanical heart valve will exert a "blender" effect that slices red cells into pieces; some patients have genetically defective red cells that self-destruct under certain circumstances; bacteria of various kinds release toxins that destroy red cells; and many different types of antibodies attack red cells. The trick is to think of the right one.

She wasn't a good historian and I had a difficult time establishing the basic facts. When did she first become ill? What symptoms did she have? Did she have pain, fever, cough or rash? When was her last normal menstrual period? Could she be pregnant? Was her current vaginal bleeding a normal period? I asked in a dozen ways about her period and about abortion, but I got nowhere. I couldn't find any answer that pointed clearly toward one thing or another. I was worried that she must have had a "coat-hanger abortion," and her uterus had become infected. I couldn't be sure.

Physical exam had been unremarkable except for the fact that she was wearing a female sanitary pad stained with dark blood. A small amount of dark blood oozed from her cervix, evidence that she could have a uterine infection associated with a back room abortion. I pressed firmly on her cervix, uterus and lower abdomen to see if she was tender. She registered only minor objection.

The internal medicine resident arrived and I told him the story. He examined her, repeated the pelvic exam, and asked some questions but learned nothing new. We stepped out of the room to talk and to my astonishment he didn't want to admit her as an internal medicine patient.

"Let the Ob-Gyn resident look at her first," he said. With that he was gone.

I spent a few minutes in the tiny nurse's office looking at a textbook of internal medicine, reading about hemolytic anemia before the OB-Gyn resident showed up. By now it was nearly midnight. He did a third pelvic exam and said he didn't think it was an Ob-Gyn problem—probably just a normal period, no pelvic tenderness or masses, blah, blah, blah—and she needed to be admitted to the floor as an internal medicine patient. Then he, too, was gone.

I called the internal medicine resident again, who by now was asleep in the call room. He was not happy to be awakened. I told him about the Ob-Gyn consultation and asked him again to admit her. He reluctantly agreed.

"You're doing fine," he said. "Put my name on her chart and I'll check her on rounds in the morning."

Which is what I did. By the time I got her into a room she was descending into coma again—whatever it was that was eating up her red cells was still doing it and had in just about two hours had destroyed most of the two units of blood I had squeezed into her. I called the lab to send a tech to collect some blood for culture, called the blood bank to order two more pints of blood. The first blood transfusions had lifter her blood pressure and expanded her veins, so I was able to get a second IV going in a vein in her arm. I gave her a massive intravenous dose of hydrocortisone and a mixture of antibiotics designed to kill any bacteria that might be the cause of the problem.

While all of this was happening I managed to get a call through to one of the phone numbers left by the people who brought her. I asked dozens of questions. Was this a normal period? Was she pregnant? Had she been sick? Was she taking any medicines? Has she been handling certain agricultural chemicals? Worrying about poisons, I asked if there been crop dusting in nearby fields in the last day or two? The answers were varieties of "No" and "Maybe" and "I don't know." I gave up. It was the middle of the night and I was a far away white man asking nosy questions about a black woman.

By the time the third and fourth pints of blood arrived she was comatose again. I squeezed the bags into her veins hoping the new red cells would relight the fires of consciousness like they had a few hours earlier. It worked. She woke up and looked around, trying to make sense of her surroundings.

Despite lack of agreement from the Ob-Gyn resident and no reliable history, I concluded she'd had a dirty abortion—her uterus and bloodstream were infected and that she was certain to die unless something, anything, could be done to change the course of events.

It was a measure of my desperation that I turned to the idea of a death-bed confession.

I said, "I am your doctor. You are going to die. But before you go, you can still get right with Jesus by answering some questions for me."

"Are you pregnant?"

She shook her head. No.

"Were you pregnant?"

Another shake. No.

"Did you try to get rid of the baby?"

No.

My hope was that if she confirmed it, I might be able to take some action—what, I couldn't exactly say—that might save her life. She denied it yet again, and died a few hours later.

I got some sleep and was at home in our little apartment behind the hospital when the phone rang. It was the pathology department. The woman's family had come for her body but it couldn't be released until someone signed the death certificate. I didn't think too much about it as I walked over to the hospital. That changed as I stared at those famous empty spaces on the bottom of every death certificate:

*Cause of death* _____

*Due to* _____

*Due to* _____

*Due to* _____

In later years, doing autopsies as a pathologist, I felt an urge to write "Birth" in the last line, but I lacked courage.

I struggled to think of what I would write. After hemming and hawing a while, I demurred, saying I needed to talk to the internal medicine resident. I found him on the internal medicine floor, but he declined to sign. He said I could write whatever I wanted; after all, I knew the patient best.

I called the pathology department and told them I couldn't sign it because I didn't know why she died. The secretary didn't seem upset about it and I went back home.

This was not what the pathology department wanted to hear. If no one would sign, then the pathology department would have to do an autopsy, so the pathologist could sign.

Word soon reached the hospital CEO and I got a call from him. I must sign that certificate, he said. There was a large family of angry blacks in the lobby who were adamantly opposed to cutting on dead bodies, and Mississippi didn't need any more trouble.

As a lowly intern, all I wanted was for the mess to go away. Nobody, it seemed, was willing to write down what killed her. I was very polite, obsequious even. I explained that I was not trying to be difficult, but I couldn't sign it because I didn't know why she died. I was very helpful sounding.

It didn't do any good. My "recalcitrance," as it was called, was most unwelcome.

I spent the rest of the afternoon at home expecting to hear again from some angry somebody at the hospital. But no call came and I went in for my 3PM–11PM shift. I called the pathology department to see what was happening and learned that the patient was being autopsied. I found my way to the morgue, where I was met with pathologists and other physicians interested in this very unusual case. Word had apparently spread. Suddenly I had become a welcome guest, at least in the morgue—I knew more about the clinical details than anyone else, even the Chief of Internal Medicine, who was standing by the autopsy table. I answered questions and explained my therapeutic approach, expecting to be challenged at every turn, but it proved to be a quiet, thoughtful assembly.

The pathologist made the usual big Y-shaped incision from each shoulder down to the lower end of the breastbone, then joined the incisions and extended it to the lower end of the abdomen. The dome of an enlarged uterus popped into view. Knowing of my suspicion of a criminal abortion, the pathologist had asked the lab to send a technologist with sterile needles, syringes and culture plates. He stuck a needle in the uterus and brought out a small amount of dark, bloody material, which he handed over to the tech.

Then he opened the uterus with a single slash: and out spilled a few ounces of malodorous, reddish-black gruel.

The next day the lab reported that the blood cultures I had collected in the emergency room and the morgue specimen contained *Clostridium perfringens*, the agent of gas gangrene. It was a virulent microbe that secreted a variety of toxins, one of which could destroy red cells. About the only thing that could cause such a problem was unsterile penetration of the uterus, such as a "coat-hanger abortion."

After the autopsy I heard no more about the case, but for a while I worried that some day angry family members might pay me a visit.

### Epilogue
Full disclosure: I support a woman's right to have an abortion and this case largely accounts for my

position. I fear cases like this one will once again be common if religious dogma succeeds in making abortion ever more difficult to obtain. Modern readers in the Age of Terror need no reminders, but religious zealotry knows no limits and accounts for much of Robert Burns' famous line: "Man's inhumanity to man makes countless thousands mourn!"

This young woman died of an infection induced by a botched amateur abortion. It has always bothered me that nothing came of it—there were no newspaper articles, no corps of reporters asking breathless questions . . . nothing . . . as there surely would have been had she been white. She deserved better.

This kind of infection was once commonly associated with ordinary childbirth. It was called puerperal sepsis, or childbed fever, and in the 17th and 18th centuries occurred as epidemics that affected about 25% of women giving birth in European hospitals. Mortality rates were high, sometimes nearly 100%. The exact cause was unknown but by 1843 Oliver Wendell Holmes, Sr., an American physician and father of the famed jurist, concluded it was infectious and recommended hand-washing and clean sheets, for which he was widely ridiculed.

The following year (1844) Ignaz Semmelweis, an Austrian obstetrician, noted that childbed fever was low in the ward where midwives delivered infants and high in the ward where physicians performed the task. The main difference was that the physicians did autopsies in the morning and came directly to the wards from the morgue, which the midwives did not do. Semmelweis ordered physicians to wash their hands in chlorinated lime solution before each delivery or vaginal examination. The mortality rate for puerperal sepsis declined from 18% to 3% in six months.

CHAPTER 5

# Trouble in Vicksburg

**Prologue**
During my six weeks in the emergency room I became entangled in a second abortion case.

Are you licensed to practice medicine in the great state of Mississippi?"

My answer—"No"—in a sleepy courtroom in Vicksburg, Mississippi in the spring of 1963, proved to be a "Perry Mason moment," a dramatic turning point when the attorney-hero nails the witness with a damning question that shifts the trial in his client's favor.

I was appearing as a witness for the state in the trial of an accused abortionist. My courtroom appearance was the culmination of a chain of events that began six months earlier in the emergency room at University

Hospital near the time my other patient had died from a botched dirty abortion. It was ten years before *Roe v. Wade* changed abortion law. In those days an induced abortion was a criminal act.

Mississippi festered with unrest in 1963. The National Guard occupied Oxford to ensure James Meredith's admission to "Ole Miss." Civil rights marches and protests were the stuff of daily news, and everyone assumed everyone else carried a gun. Nevertheless, the emergency room wasn't the bee-hive of activity portrayed in modern TV dramas. It was a small space with a few exam/treatment rooms on either side of a short hallway. During the day and early evening it was populated by a few nurses and interns. Late at night and in the small hours of the morning a solo nurse and intern were sufficient.

Most cases were not emergencies, so we spent the better part of our time dealing with feverish infants, broken bones, mystery pains and various other ordinary medical problems. Though lacking in drama most of the time, one of the attractions of emergency medicine is that you never know what will roll through the door.

Such was the case about midnight in the fall of 1962. The nurse told me she had a patient ready for me to see, a young woman with "cramps and heavy vaginal bleeding."

I found a sweaty, apprehensive young woman with a mop of short dark hair sitting on the edge of the exam table in an exam gown with a sheet draped over her lap.  She was attractive and articulate—a well-bred southern girl of the type whose parents could afford orthodontists, tennis lessons, and private schools. The chart indicated that she was from Vicksburg, sixty miles to the west of Jackson.  Naïf that I was, it did not strike me as unusual that an eighteen-year old girl was in our emergency room, far from home and without her mother, for a rather ordinary medical problem.

I asked the usual questions, but didn't learn much beyond what I could see and what the nurse noted in her interview.  I called the nurse to be present while I did a vaginal exam.

To my astonishment, the girl's vagina was packed with a long, bloody strip of gauzy cotton tape, the type used by surgeons to pack around a surgical work area to soak up blood.  I gently tugged it out to reveal a coiled, stiff, red rubber catheter deep in her vagina, its tip inserted into the mouth of her uterus.  I recognized it immediately for what it was: a fairly safe method to irritate the uterus and induce labor.  It was working. She was having an induced—and illegal—abortion. My next thought was that the day would come when my notes—and maybe I—would be in court.

I called the Ob-Gyn resident.  He judged the process was too far along to try to halt without chancing serious infection or other complication, and admitted her for the standard procedure in such cases: open the mouth of the uterus and scrape out the products of conception. Certain that the catheter and the chart would show up in court, I told the nurse to save the catheter and I made unusually detailed notes.

I forgot about it until spring when I was subpoenaed to testify. The trial was to be in Vicksburg, where the abortion had been instigated. I spoke by phone with the prosecutor's office, which made clear to me that I was to be a fact witness and was not to issue any medical opinions.

On the appointed day I was shown to the witness room, a small second floor space overlooking the street. It was a hot day and the window was open. I leaned out to catch a breeze and noticed a liquor store across the street. Never mind that the state was legally dry.

It will convey a sense of the state of the law in Mississippi in those days that my wife and I bought our monthly bottle of Old Crow bourbon a few miles outside of Jackson at a warehouse-sized building set back in the pines off a two-lane blacktop. The proprietor made half-hearted gestures to avoid offending the sensibilities of the constabulary and law-abiding citizens by pretending to operate a legitimate business. Facing the road was a poor imitation of a convenience store. A faded sign stood out front with a dim interior sporting a few shelves littered by dusty cans and boxes. Around back, however, was a paved and well-lighted parking lot. Inside the door was a small bare room with a clean counter, no cash register, no merchandize, no clock, and no signs, not even one stating "Cash Only." Customers announced their want, an unsmiling attendant nodded and disappeared into the back, and soon reappeared with a brown paper sack, which was briefly held open for the customer's inspection of the contents. Exact cash was required. Asking for change was considered the mark of a newcomer or troublemaker. Everyone knew the prices and the rules. Cash was tendered and that was it. It must have been a gold mine.

The store across the street from the Vicksburg courthouse required no such impositions. Customers entered through a shiny, windowed storefront beneath a large, welcoming "Liquor" sign.

As I tried to wrap my mind around the realities of liquor stores in a dry state and the differing lawless practices between Jackson and Vicksburg, a lawman stopped in for a visit. A big gold badge announced "Sheriff." He was outfitted in a carefully tailored tan shirt and trousers with sharp military creases, and topped by a tan hat with a narrow, turned up brim. Completing the picture was a heavy Sam Browne belt with thick shoulder strap, the better to tote the huge pistol at his waist.

"You must be the doctor," he said, offering his huge hand. He was big, not merely fat, and his heft and growling voice suggested carnivorous power.

We shook. "Yes, sir," I said, "I'm the doctor." His comment implied I was the only one. I'd been worried that some other doctor might be there to testify that I had made stupid mistakes.

"I'm the sheriff," he said. "Since this, uh, incident took place out in the county it's in my jurisdiction. I like to keep close track of my cases. No surprises, you know."

"Yes, sir," I said.

He sat down. I leaned on the window sill. He asked a few questions about the case. His questions were direct, and while not unfriendly, they were not designed to put me, a guest in his courthouse, at ease. I gathered that he was used to saying what he pleased and being indulged by listeners. I didn't know much about such things, but his questions seemed aimed to find out what I was going to say on the witness stand. It made me uncomfortable, so I sought to redirect the conversation.

Finding it richly ironic that an illegal business openly operated on a street corner across from the local temple of justice, I ventured a question.

"Is it true," I asked, just to be certain my understanding of the law was correct, "that liquor sales are illegal in Mississippi."

"Yep, son, that's the law."

"How, then, can it be that there's a liquor store across the street from the courthouse?" I asked, pointing out the window.

"Well, son, the citizens are gonna drink," he said, sliding down in his chair, legs outstretched, admiring the gleam on his spit-polished boots. "You're a doctor and all, and I figure you've seen more than a few broke up drunks over there in Jackson at your new hospital. Now ain't I right?"

"Yes, sir," I said. "We see our share."

"And you see that bridge over there," he said, still studying his boots. The big bridge across the Mississippi River was not far beyond the courthouse.

"Yes, sir, it's hard to miss," I said.

"Well, son, at the other end of that bridge is the state of Louisiana. You cross that bridge and no sooner than your wheels take one turn on Cajun soil you're gonna find a liquor store. Mississippians will have their liquor and it's mighty close by. No point in making our folks drive to Louisiana to get their booze," he said. "Besides, that liquor store pays a lot of taxes. No point in them Cajuns collecting money we could keep here in Vicksburg."

I couldn't grasp how an illegal business could be taxed. "How is it that you can tax something that doesn't exist in the eyes of the law?" I asked.

A cloud of irritation passed over his face. He fixed me with a scowl and pushed himself upright in the chair.

Seeking to relieve the tension, I tried to make light of my comment. "So what would happen," I asked, "if that legally non-existent liquor store decided to pay taxes in equally non-existent imaginary dollars?" Fool that I was, I expected he would get a chuckle out of it.

"Son," he growled, and stood up, "we don't have them problems here in Vicksburg. Everybody here does what they 's supposed to."

He hefted his belt and holster for comfort and strode out. "I'll see you in the courtroom," he said.

Was that a threat? Was there more to this case than an abortion? Lost in thought, it finally dawned on me who collected the "taxes" paid by the liquor store. It was a relief to hear the bailiff call my name.

The courtroom was a southern classic—a somber, airless, place that suggested stern justice tempered with little mercy. The floor was formed of straight pine boards, and dark wood paneling covered the walls. The lighting was poor and the ceiling was high to accommodate a balcony, where blacks were seated. Gauzy white drapes hung limply in tall, open windows, and ceiling fans turned slowly, barely disturbing air so thick with heat and humidity that it seemed liquid.

I took the witness stand, the judge on my right and an all-white, all male jury on my left. I quickly scanned the courtroom to identify the players. At one table sat a well-dressed middle-aged, black woman and three well-groomed lawyers with polished briefcases and orderly stacks of papers—the alleged abortionist and her lawyers. I searched for the victim but couldn't find her. Only later did I learn she was the perfectly appointed, newly blonde young woman on the front row.

At the other table sat a small man with thin, unkempt gray hair and a rumpled seersucker suit—the prosecutor. After I was sworn in, he stumbled around asking me questions about who I was, where I got my education, about my job as an intern in Jackson, and so on. His questions belied an ignorance of how doctors are educated and trained. At one point he asked if my answers indicated that they meant that I was "a real doctor." I suspected he wasn't sure and really wanted to know. He led me through a recitation of the events of the evening in question and showed me my emergency room notes and the catheter for identification.

Finally he said, "Your witness," and one of the defense lawyers came forward. He introduced himself and asked a single question. "*Doctor* McConnell," he said, with sarcastic emphasis, "are you licensed to practice medicine in the great state of Mississippi?"

"No," I replied. A collective gasp rose from the courtroom. In an indelible instant I had become another meddling outsider like civil rights workers, like Martin Luther King, like the National Guard and the mob of FBI agents and federal marshals who swarmed into the state to insure, among other things, that James Meredith, the first black to enroll at Ole Miss, remained enrolled.

"No more questions, your honor," he said with a flourish and returned to his seat.

For what seemed an eternity, nobody said or did anything. The place was paralyzed by the revelation. I might as well have been unmasked as a voodoo doctor from the alien reaches of south Louisiana who had infiltrated the sanctity of Mississippi sovereignty to treat patients by sacrificing a black rooster and saying incantations before adorning the patient with a gris-gris bag containing a possum snout and an alligator tooth.

I looked to the prosecutor, expecting him to explore the nature of the "institutional permit" system under which interns and residents move from one state to another for training without having to take state licensing exams. But he, too, looked dumb-founded. Searching for a way to end the agony of silence, I looked to the judge, who appeared as befuddled as the prosecutor.

"Your honor," I began helpfully, "it's not necessary for me to have a license because …"

Recovering his balance, the judge dismissed me with a wave of his hand. "Son," he said, pointing to the jury box, "tell yo' story to the jury," with emphasis on "story." In a stroke I was reduced to child in short pants trying to explain away some mischief.

I turned to face twelve white males, whose faces suggested dynamite-blasted granite more than human flesh. Not one to be deterred in most situations, I plunged on. I owe much of my position in life to an ability to sell my ideas, and myself, so I adopted my most helpful, earnest and conciliatory manner and began to explain. I avoided big words and dropped down as far as legitimately possible into the southern vernacular as I explained the process of medical education. I told of my college education, medical school, and internship. I explained institutional permits, the latter a kind of temporary license good only while working in a hospital that trains new doctors. I thought they would surely understand that my motives for being in Mississippi were virtuous. I had been to a fine university, had four years of medical school, graduating near the top of my class, and I was healing the sick for a pauper's wage in their fine state university hospital. And, finally, they would understand the necessity of institutional permits and how the system benefited every Mississippian.

With every word it seemed more and more lame. I knew it was over. Finally, I turned to the prosecutor, hoping he would ask some helpful questions to rescue the situation. The defense lawyers looked smug; the prosecutor just sat there. The judge told me I was dismissed, and I skulked back to Jackson, where the bootleggers at least had a sense of decorum.

I learned the next day that the verdict was not guilty.

## Epilogue

Given the circumstances—a crime involving a young white female, a black defendant being tried before an all white, all male jury amid the poisonous racial unrest and violence in Mississippi in 1963—more than a few who learn of this story are surprised by the jury's "Not Guilty" verdict. I was at the time.

But nearly fifty years later a different perspective emerges.

What modern readers fail to understand is the social context of abortion before the Roe v. Wade decision by the U. S. Supreme Court (1973), which legalized most abortions.

By strict medical definition an abortion is interruption of pregnancy before 20 weeks or 500 grams (1 lb, 2 oz) fetal weight. Among the lay public, however, "abortion" universally means induced (voluntary) abortion, and spontaneous (involuntary) abortion is called "miscarriage."

Before Roe v. Wade almost every induced abortion was a criminal act. At the time every state banned abortion, with some exceptions: to save the life of the mother, in cases of rape or incest, or if the fetus was deformed. As a consequence, almost every induced abortion was performed outside of the traditional medical establishment, often with dire consequences for the mother. "A Death in Jackson" is an example.

Unwanted pregnancies were as common then as now. In my six weeks duty in the emergency room I had this case and the fatal case described earlier. Unmarried pregnancy was accompanied by social stigmatization as damning as wearing a Scarlet Letter. So it should be no surprise that the nation was served by a shadowy legion of abortionists, with one in virtually every community. They were tolerated, even sheltered, like bootleggers during Prohibition, as a necessary solution to law not in tune with public need.

I have often wondered if the District Attorney purposefully assigned a stumblebum assistant DA to represent the state, especially against the polished defense team. The State's case was hobbled—I was a State's witness: a mere juvenile among the greybeards in the jury box and, *quelle horreur,* a non-Mississippian. In retrospect the Not Guilty verdict seems foreordained. Everybody won. The girl got on with her life, the abortionist was spared conviction, and abortion remained available in reasonably safe hands.

CHAPTER 6

# Remembering
# Sylvester Parham

**Prologue**
   While an extern at Timberlawn I had concluded
psychiatry was not what I wanted to do.  But I had not
yet decided whether or not to choose pathology.  The
internal debate continued during my internship year.

The enduring appeal of clinical medicine is, of
course, the patients.  Nevertheless, I became a
pathologist.  Apart from laboratory research, pathology is about as far from direct patient contact as practicing medicine allows.
   Pathology attracted me in my sophomore year of
medical school.  I had excelled at anatomy and physiology as a freshman, and pathology was nothing more
than anatomy and physiology gone wrong.  It was fun

to study, I made good grades, and the professors gave me attention that was flattering.  Satisfying though it was, like every other medical student I eagerly antici- pated the junior and senior years, during which we were to rotate through surgery, obstetrics and gyne- cology, pediatrics, internal medicine, psychiatry and a few specialty electives.  Eager though I was, I was wary. I had watched general practice in a small town con- sume my father.  He was a solo practitioner in a time when the doctor was always on call.  And he had other problems—a toxic mix of smoking, drug addiction and alcohol abuse.  I was certain the stress of patient care contributed to his death when he was forty-seven.

During my third and fourth years of medical school I found it difficult to confront the harsh reali- ties of severe, deforming, or crippling disease.  It was not revulsion.  Rather it was the stark reality of my vul- nerability to the terrible conditions I encountered: dis- figuring burns; neck fractures with complete paralysis, and throat cancer patients breathing through a hole in their neck.  Pathology, on the other hand, was appeal- ing because I loved the science and it didn't require confronting such unpleasant realities.

As an intern I was still low on the clinical totem pole, but I relished the expanded responsibility and the authority and freedom of action that came with it. The drama and intimacy of direct patient care was not as glamorous as modern TV medical soap operas—it was decidedly more gritty, compelling and seductive.

By the middle of my internship year I was questioning my earlier thoughts about pathology or some form of clinical medicine.  Late at night in the subdued light of hospital corridors or the rooms of sleeping patients, I would rewind the mental tape and replay the debate.

The matter crystallized when I was on my general surgery rotation.  I was assisting two resident surgeons exploring the pelvis of one of my patients, a man with a large bladder cancer.  Actually, I was just standing there like a stump, holding a retractor, but I had a clear view of what was happening.  The surgery residents were deep in the man's pelvis on a mission to remove his bladder.  Our patient began to bleed briskly—blood welled up into the wound at an alarming rate from some source deeper than we could see.  The residents couldn't get it stopped.  They'd suction it out, trying to see exactly where it was coming from, but as soon as they cleared it away more appeared.

By the tone of their voices I could tell desperation was mounting, but they were reluctant to call a faculty surgeon.  While desperation mounted I recalled some things I'd read preparing myself for the case.  I'd boned up on the anatomy of the bladder and pelvis, which included some illustrations of the blood supply.  Thus armed and feeling bullet-proof like most 24 year old males, I decided to make a suggestion, worried all the while that as the lowest of the low in the room that all I would earn was scorn.  Why didn't they temporarily clamp off a certain artery, I suggested, it's right down there, I said, pointing to the spot where the anatomy books said it ought to be. They could then mop up the blood, loosen the clamp a bit and identify the source of the bleeding, stop it and then remove the clamp. They clamped and the bleeding stopped. They found the bleeder and the remainder of the surgery proceeded as planned.

I thought little more of it until a few days later I was summoned to the surgery chairman's office. I couldn't imagine why, but it couldn't be good. I was being called on the carpet; that was certain. Imagine my surprise when he referred to the case and appealed to me to become a surgery resident in his program after my internship year. I was flattered and began to consider the possibility.

Then along came Sylvester Parham. Though it is a violation of the usual ethic, I am remembering him by name because I wonder if anyone other than me, even his own family, remembers this poor, young black man from rural Mississippi gone now nearly fifty years. Sylvester can never know how he affected me. He died while in my care. Even had he survived, for me to say "thank you" would be not the right sentiment.

Sylvester was nineteen, out of high school a year. He had just bought his first car. His mother told me how he loved having that old car even though it always needed tinkering to keep it going. One fine spring day of 1963 Sylvester and a friend were cleaning out the fuel line. Sylvester, bending over the engine end of the line, cigarette in his mouth, asked his buddy back at the gas tank to "blow on it" to clean out the line. The spray of gasoline covered Sylvester and he exploded in flames.

I first saw him in the emergency room. I had seen burns before, but nothing this bad, nor this fresh. He was delirious with pain, hair and eyebrows burned away, the pink under-surface of his black skin revealed, the remainder blistered and hanging in shreds that called to mind Shakespeare's line from King Lear, "a looped and windowed raggedness." The only unburned skin was around his genitals, in the crease of his buttocks, where his shoes had covered his feet, and where his belt fitted around his waist. The smell of burned flesh and hair was awful. It was all I could do to stay in the room. I wanted to run, not because the sight, the smell, or his screams were too much for my senses, but because I could not bear being on intimate terms with such agony and tragedy. It was too easy to put myself in his place.

He was admitted to a regular hospital room; burn units were rare in those days. I was assigned to the team caring for him. His mother brought a picture of him and propped it in the window of his room. He was a robust, handsome, young man, only a few years younger than me, but I could not match his face to the grotesque mask that lay nearby. I tried to be optimistic, to pump up his spirits and hers, but I wasn't very good at deception. I knew, and I'm certain she knew, he was going to die. Within a week his burns became terribly infected with a bacterium that stimulates copious amounts of malodorous, thick, green pus. I found it almost impossible to go into his room. But his mother came every day and she never flinched. In the face of such courage only the shame of cowardice drove me through the door and into his room each day to confront my inadequacy and his agony.

Sylvester lived thirty terrible days in the hospital and I was with him much of the time. By the time he died I had was certain I could never be a surgeon or practice any other discipline that offered much chance of having a case that would so overwhelm me. I was never tempted again by clinical medicine.


### Epilogue

And so I became a pathologist. The practice of pathology is a dry sandwich, larded only with the occasional misadventures of our clinical brethren, whom we serve daily instead of patients. We salve our bruised egos with the idea that we are "the doctor's doctor" but that gets the relationship exactly upside down. Clinicians are our masters. We are at their beck and call, and hearing a kind word for a job well done is not part of the usual relationship. But we accumulate a few stories. Clinicians can make fools or heroes of themselves in an endless variety of ways, but they aren't nearly so compelling as patients.

CHAPTER 7

# In the JFK Funeral

**Prologue**

After finishing my internship in June 1963, I joined the Army. It was an easy decision.  I knew I'd have to serve two years at one time or another. The US military  would not become an all-volunteer force until 1973, events in Vietnam were heating up, and the military draft was in full operation.  The odds of getting drafted were relatively low for most guys, but not for doctors.  The military allowed us to defer our service for specialty training, but I wanted to get it out of the way.  What's more, I was flat broke and owed a few hundred dollars from the birth of our first child.  Compared to the $165 a month I was paid as an intern, the prospect of $525 a month as a military doctor was very appealing.

After spending some time at a special school for new military doctors at Fort Sam Houston in San Antonio, I was assigned to be a general medical officer in the Pentagon Dispensary.

When the phone rang I had my finger up a colonel's ass, examining his prostate. I was an Army doc in my office at the Pentagon doing an annual physical exam on one of the many in the Pentagon who appeared daily in the dispensary for minor ailments and general checkups. It was Friday, November 22, 1963.

I shucked the glove and answered the phone. Nobody but Marianne would be calling on that line. She said that it was all over television that shots had been fired at President Kennedy during his trip to Dallas. I cautioned her not to spread such a rumor because I was liable to propagate it. She was trying to convince me that it was serious when the phone went dead. Weeks later my next-door neighbor, a junior Naval Intelligence officer who worked deep underground in the Pentagon, told me that all casual phone lines to the Pentagon had been cut..

Normality ceased. Helicopters filled the air and people ran down the halls. In the clinic, we cancelled all appointments, turned on the waiting room TV and like everyone else we watched as Walter Cronkite gave us the news that Kennedy was dead.

I called my best friend from medical school, Don Payne, who was stationed nearby as Chief Medical Officer for the Military District of Washington, which was in charge of the military aspect of all manner of things in the District of Columbia, including state funerals. Don, always a charming schemer, assured me he could get us posted to the White House as a medical detail. But, as with all things with Don, I took it with a grain of salt. This time, however, it proved no boast. The next morning Don called to say I would be on the team to support the funeral.

I imagined a bunch of military doctors, some nurses and medics and a senior officer in command. We would deploy to the White House and blanket it with our expertise. Wrong. It was just Don and me. Some anonymous power from above posted us to the White House, to the Capitol, and to Arlington National Cemetery with the general idea that it would be good to have some physicians around. Our orders were vague, which worried me initially, but Don, with typical panache, opined that we would play it by ear. And so we did. We spent three memorable days at the epicenter of the Kennedy funeral in large part because things were so unstructured. We had unsupervised run of the places we visited. Waving those orders around was magic.

The afternoon of Saturday, November 23, outfitted in dark green dress uniform, tan shirt and black tie, we were taken to the White House in a military police car. We were waved through the gate and up the circular drive to the North Portico. The doors were flung open with snappy salutes by the military on duty, and we went inside.

Our initial duty was to stand in the East Room while crowds of dignitaries filed by. I walked around in a daze, trying to take in the enormity of what was happening. Within a few minutes I found lying on a table nearby a newspaper from 1865 open to several drawings of the East Room, as it had been for Lincoln's funeral. The black crepe draping around me was arrayed in exactly the same way. The casket was positioned in the center of the room, and guarded by four honor guardsmen, one each from the four uniformed services. The casket was closed by order of Mrs. Kennedy, who had visited earlier in the day.

I stood by the door as guests entered from the Green Room, which joins the south end of the East Room. Much of the Kennedy clan came through at one time or another. The only snatch of conversation I recall from any of the guests was Bobby Kennedy discussing plans for a JFK memorial with Kennedy brother in-law Sargent Shriver. They paused at the door, deep in conversation, oblivious to my presence a few feet away. I was a bit taken aback by the topic, feeling that it was time for mourning, not for planning monuments.

At one point we took a break in the State Dining Room, which is on the main floor with the East Room, but on the west side. It was laid out for a buffet with white tablecloths and White House dinnerware. I don't recall the details of the imprint on the silver or china other than thinking it would be a nice memento to spirit away a plate, but visions of courts martial squelched the idea. Besides, my mother would have been horrified. We had tea and finger sandwiches served by a black butler in formal wear who had served every president since Herbert Hoover. I tried to draw out on some tidbits from his White House tenure, but he would have none of it.

After the break Don went back to the East Room and, because the crowds were thin and I wasn't needed, I wandered about. It was amazing. Nobody was home. Think about it: Kennedy was dead and Lyndon Johnson, not wanting to appear too eager to seize the reins of office, had decided to delay moving in. The grand stairs to the upper floor, the President's private quarters, were unguarded and beckoning. I might be able to say I once lay abed in the Lincoln Bedroom. I took a few steps upward and stopped. Mother would not approve of such shameless voyeurism. So, I retreated and headed for the West Wing.

Expecting with every step to be confronted by a Secret Service agent, I walked down the colonnade past the Rose Garden toward the Oval Office. It was eerily quiet, the silence offended only by my breathing and the soft footfalls of my spit-polished black shoes. The nation, it seemed, was holding its breath.

The first door on the left in the West Wing opened onto the hall that leads to the Oval Office. Down the short hall I could see the famous blue carpet glowing through the open door.

To my immediate left was the door to the Cabinet Room, also standing open. I stepped inside and admired the huge table and big chairs, then retreated back to the hall and walked a few more steps toward the Oval Office. A souvenir would be nice. Once again, I couldn't do it. To use a national calamity as an excuse to ogle the sanctity of a national institution was more than my conscience could bear. Looking back, I should have taken the Don Payne approach: march in like you belong, take an ashtray or pen and swagger away.

I returned to the East Room and conferred with Don. We decided it was time to go home. But exactly how do you go home, to a tiny apartment in Arlington, Virginia, from the White House? We didn't know what to do because we hadn't made arrangements. While musing out loud about how to make our escape, Kennedy's Chief of Protocol, Angier Biddle Duke, walked by with an admiral. They were discussing their need for a limousine. Don, always the opportunist, suggested we follow the Ambassador as he went down the stairs to the ground floor. Soon we found ourselves standing in line to use a very important telephone. Everyone seemed to be a general, admiral, or ambassador of some sort, and we blended right in with our dress uniforms. When Mr. Duke's turn came he said, "This is Ambassador Duke. I need a car at the North Portico." Following his lead, when our turn came Don took the phone and said, "This is Captain Payne. Captain McConnell and I need a car at the North Portico for transport to the Pentagon." He didn't say we were lowly Army Captains, not near the equivalent of the Navy rank.

We made our way to the North Portico and soon a military police car rolled up and our names were called. Honor guardsmen rushed to open the doors, salutes were exchanged and away we went.

Sunday, November 24, the president's body was taken to the Capitol rotunda to lie in state. I was assigned to work an evening shift and be available if anyone in the throng of public mourners needed medical attention. By then I had learned more of the workings of things and knew to call the Pentagon motor pool and requisition a car. Wanting some company, I talked to my next-door neighbor, the naval intelligence officer, and he agreed to come along and pretend to be my assistant.

We appeared at the designated place in the Pentagon parking lot and were met by a military police detail that included a driver and another soldier, plus military motorcycle outriders. Off we went, traveling east along Independence Avenue, the Mall and Washington Monument on our left, lights flashing. The motorcycles sped ahead, stopping traffic at intersections between the Pentagon and the Capitol, each of which also was guarded by armed military.

As we neared the Capitol we encountered more traffic and soon were nosing our way through the immense throng assembled to pay their respects. The Capitol parking lot, which in those days separated the east face of the Capitol from the Supreme Court, was closed and the crowd pressed against the fence as they funneled into the lot from the sole open gate across from the Supreme Court. Our entrance, however, was to be at a southern gate, which was blocked by the crowd. With some difficulty the motorcycle escorts parted the crowd, which pressed against the windows of our car, cameras flashing, as if rock stars were inside. Finally, the gates swung open to reveal a long line of mourners edging across the otherwise empty lot and up the steps into the rotunda. It was then that it hit me: I didn't know where to go. After such an entrance, we couldn't just get out of the car and get in line.

The only thing I could think to do was to tell the driver to take us to the side of the steps, where I could see a door. The car rolled to a stop and once again the doors were flung open with salutes, accompanied by murmuring and camera flashes from the crowd. We got out and strode purposefully under the steps as if we knew what we were doing. After the military police were gone we explored a bit and found our way through the door and up several levels to the Rotunda.

The casket, draped with the Stars and Stripes, stood in the center. Posted at the corners were guards, one from each branch of the military. They stood facing the casket, heads bowed, hands resting on their rifles, still as stone. Stationed nearby was an artist commissioned to capture the scene in oils on a big canvas. The throng of mourners shuffled by in streams on each side, hushed and respectful. It was quiet enough to hear sighs and sobs.

Medically, the evening was quiet. My only casualty was a drunken young man who had tried unsuccessfully to climb the iron fence around the parking lot and had had fallen on one of the spikes, which jabbed him in the anus.

I don't recall how we got home.

I returned alone to the Capitol on Monday, November 25. My duty station was to the south side at the top of the same steps and directly above the entrance I'd used the night before. There is a famous photo of Jackie, veiled in black, at the top of those steps as she is exiting the rotunda, children at her side, looking out at the crowd. I am captured in some photographs of the scene standing to her right with a crew from NBC news.

Earlier, before Jackie's appearance, I had taken up a conversation with a reporter from NBC News, Nancy Dickerson. I foolishly told her I was from Dallas, which occasioned some sharp questioning by a professional questioner. But she was courteous and to my relief put her headphones back on as I stood by silently taking in the scene. Suddenly she put her hands to her earphones, pressing them tightly to her head, and began shaking her head. Then she ripped the phones off and turned to me, furious. I recall her words exactly: "What kind of people are you down there in Dallas!" It wasn't a question, but a judgment: she had just heard that Jack Ruby had shot Lee Harvey Oswald in the basement of the Dallas jail. I don't recall what I said.

After the casket was carried down the steps, the cortege formed and began its slow pace up Pennsylvania Avenue on its way to Arlington National Cemetery. Somehow, I don't recall how, I wound up at the Cemetery standing by the grave site. There wasn't much for me to do, so I just stood there, trying to look official and dignified, and watched world leaders file by. The most memorable was Charles DeGaulle, resplendent in his military uniform. He was imposing. Not just tall, he was big, with an arching belly and massive shoulders. Sir Alec Douglas Hume, the Queen's Prime Minister, also passed by. Many had familiar faces, but I could not put names with them. Again, there was little for me to do, so I took a lot of pictures. I had only one patient, a bemedaled Army Green Beret, swaying in the otherwise perfectly still alignment of the honor guard that lined the walkway. He looked like he needed help, so I went over to see about him. He was staggering drunk.

# CHAPTER 8

# Jumping for Joy

## Prologue

Despite the drama of the Kennedy funeral, I did not like being a general medical officer in the Pentagon dispensary. It was numbingly dull and I hated wearing the required dress uniform with starched shirt and tie. I wanted to wear the comfortable fatigues we wore during training classes in the summer. As much as I hated the dress uniform, I hated more the bus ride to work. The very idea of riding a bus was alien, and by the time the bus got to my stop it was full, and I had to stand all the way in my stiff, uncomfortable uniform. I found a way out.

Did he say "Go!" or "No!"? I hesitated. Should I jump or not? The scene a thousand feet below was peaceful, even inviting.

Go or No? It was impossible to know for sure amid the chaos. To my right two big turboprop engines screamed, cold air whistled across the open door, vibrating metal clattered, and the jumpers behind me were shouting. Out of the corner of my eye I saw the light on the left side of the door flash from red to green. The pilot had cleared us to jump, but it had been hammered into my head at jump school that the final signal came from the jumpmaster.

No or Go? The distinction was important. Honored as the lead jumper, I had the duty to set an example. Hesitation was dishonor. My mind raced. This was my first jump. What did I know? If the pilot had brought us in too high and I led the others out the door, we might drift away from the drop zone and land in the river. If we were too low we might hit the ground before our parachutes opened. If the wind was too high it might drag us into the trees. If my static line was wrapped around my ankle I would dangle in the slipstream, slapping the fuselage, until the jumpmaster cut me loose. As I tumbled away it would be up to me to jerk the ripcord to open the small reserve parachute strapped across my chest.

Apart from the tension of the moment, I was happy to have found a way to get out of the stultifying routine of the Pentagon. I had asked my commanding officer how to get out. "Volunteer for the airborne and rangers," he said. "It's hard for them to find doctors stupid enough to do all of that crap." I volunteered immediately.

I reported to jump school in February 1964 and found myself one of the few junior officers in a training company of about 100 mostly teenaged enlisted men under the vigilant glare of a sinewy black taskmaster who introduced himself as "Moon Pie" Rucker. "I am the oldest man in this company," he said. "You do not have permission to be tired until I am tired."

Days were long and hellish. Breakfast at 5:30 AM, a long run at 6:00, training all day in various arenas, and countless pushups for the slightest infraction, most of them impossible to avoid.

"Captain McConnell," Sergeant Rucker liked to say to me, "how can an educated man like you be so damned stupid? Give me twenty." The proper response was "Yes, sergeant. No excuses, sergeant," and snap out twenty precise pushups.

Junior officers like me trained with enlisted personnel, and the sergeants loved their temporary dominion over us. And woe to the jumper, officer or not, who stood out from the crowd for any reason. Absolute conformity and obedience was the order of the day. In our group was a young Navy lieutenant, a scholarship gymnast, who was headed for the rigors of Navy Seal training. During our first morning in the rope pit he made the mistake of demonstrating his prowess. Our job was to climb a thick rope, slap the bar at the top to get some lampblack on our fingers, slide back down, and show our black fingers to Sergeant Rucker. Climbing a rope is hard—very hard—I barely made it to the top.  Mr. Seal, however, sat down, grabbed one rope in each hand, and with legs extended perfectly, ratcheted himself to the top, grabbed the bar, did about a dozen pull-ups, and rappelled back down.  It was a spectacular feat, which left the rest of us agog.  Sergeant Rucker, however, was not pleased.

The next morning he assigned Mr. Navy Seal to run in circles around the company as we jogged in formation.  The task in the cold early dark of a Georgia morning was made a fraction easier by singing the WWII classic "Blood on the Risers" to the tune of "The Battle Hymn of the Republic."

*He was just a rookie trooper and he surely shook with fright*
*He checked off his equipment and made sure his pack was tight;*
*He had to sit and listen to those awful engines roar,*
*"You ain't gonna jump no more!"*

*Gory, gory, what a helluva way to die,*
*Gory, gory, what a helluva way to die,*
*Gory, gory, what a helluva way to die,*
*He ain't gonna jump no more!*

It was a murderously taxing task, the equivalent of endless wind sprints, but the kid seemed unfazed.  He should have faked being tired.

Rucker made a further point at our next stop, the
Falling Pit, where we learned the fine art of the parachute landing fall, or PLF, as we called it. Yes, in the US
Army there is a right way and a wrong way to fall down
after landing in your parachute. Along one side of the
pit was an elevated platform where aspiring jumpers
stood in full harness, tethered by a rope to a beam
high in front of the platform. The thing looked like a
mass gallows, but without trap doors. Victims jumped
off, swung out over the pit, oscillating back and forth.
A drill sergeant kept them aloft by holding onto a rope
that ran through the pulley. After a few swings the sergeant would let go of the rope and dump them to the
ground at the bottom of an arc, simulating the lateral
drift of most parachute landings. Proper technique
for a PLF called for turning under the lead shoulder
to roll, feet flying overhead. Properly executed, your
feet arced over to meet the ground and momentum
or, in an actual jump, your billowing chute pulled you
upright.

Mr. Navy Seal dutifully perched on the edge.
Sergeant Rucker held the rope and gave the order,
"Go!" Mr. Seal jumped, leaping forward as far as he
could to get a bigger swing than anyone else. And so
he did. He swung out, far out, and back, smiling like
a child in a swing, until Sergeant Rucker let go of the
rope at the top end of the next traverse. Mr. Seal arced
out as if tossed by a giant hand and landed with a dull
thud. Nobody moved. Rucker said, "Oops" and stood

aside for another instructor. For the first time our Seal didn't leap up. Finally, he got to his feet. I could see by the look on his face that he'd learned the lesson.

The most feared training drill was the Tower, dubbed "The Great Separator" because more trainees chickened-out there than anywhere else, including airplane jumps. It was like a modern amusement park zip line, a high cage with long cables that reached to the ground about 100 yards away. Trainees jumped, falling free in bungee-jump fashion, and slid down the cable until their feet hit the ground, where they were to execute a parachute-landing fall. You'd think jumping out of an airplane would be scarier. It's not. In a plane you're too high to feel the height; not so the Tower.

Then the time came for our first jump from an airplane. In typical Army fashion we harnessed up, 'chutes and reserves clipped on, and sat for hours waiting for word to be radioed in from the drop zone that conditions were right. I inspected the packing tag on my chute. On it was the name of the rigger—Whiteside. I wondered who he was and if he was alive. Riggers packed the 'chutes and once a month had to jump in a random one with their name on it. Finally, the word came and we boarded up, two groups of about a dozen jumpers each, one to each side of the cargo hold of a big turboprop transport. We flew around for about an hour while the pilots did navigation drills and we contemplated life and death.

Finally, the jumpmaster shouted, "Six minutes out!" He heaved open the big doors on each side and tilted out a little platform at the bottom to form a ledge where the first jumper was to stand, shielded from hurricane-force wind by the curve of the fuselage. Screaming wind was added to rattle and roar.

"Two minutes!" I perched on the edge of my seat, ready for the next command.

"Stand up!" I faced the rear of the aircraft and the jumpmaster a few feet away, legs wide, braced against the turbulence. For the first time I noticed that jumpmasters wore Air Force parachutes with a ripcord handle. No girly static line for them. If he got sucked out the door he had to deploy the 'chute himself.

"Hook up!" I gripped the thick, yellow cord attached to my 'chute, slapped the clip onto the cable that ran above my head, and gave it a wiggle to ensure it would slide with me to the door. The static line ran over my shoulder to the 'chute pack on my back, where it attached to pins that held in place heavy cloth flaps that embraced the 'chute. As the jumper fell way from the plane the static line jerked out the pins and the flaps sprang open to release a carefully folded bundle of nylon, which in a perfect world always blossomed into a smooth round canopy.

"Check static line!" I inspected the clip to be certain the clasp had closed properly, and inserted the cotter pin to lock it shut.

"Sound off for static line check!" From the back of the line came a series of OKs followed by a slap to the thigh of the jumper in front. When the slap reached me I added my OK with what I hoped was inspiring confidence to the troops I was to lead out the door.

"Equipment check!" I inspected what I could see of my gear, especially the reserve 'chute clipped onto my chest and the clasps on top of each shoulder that held the main 'chute straps to the harness. The jumper behind me, after finishing his own inspection, clapped me on the shoulder. I turned around to inspect his static line and main 'chute pack; static line free of entanglement, pins inserted correctly, hook-up okay. I felt the jumpmaster checking out my pack. With a final shoulder slap we turned back toward the doors.

"Sound off for equipment check!" A series of OKs chorused forward.

"Shuffle to the door!" I shuffled forward, the others pressed close behind me. The jumpmaster leaned out the door looking through the slipstream to the drop zone. The rush of air distorted his face as he looked for the smoke grenade that marked the near edge of the drop zone.

"Stand in the door!" That was a command to me alone. After I jumped the others would follow at a quickstep run. I put my feet on the platform and extended my arms, flattening my palms on the cold metal skin of the plane. The only thing that kept me from being blown away was the curve of the fuselage.

The light on the left side of the door glowed red. For all of the bedlam, it was a beautiful and peaceful scene. The sun was half down behind the trees. In the condensing dusk below a jeep, ambulance, and transport trucks sat, toy-like, at the edge of a large clearing. Grenade smoke drifted lazily.

Go or No? Paralyzed by indecision, I looked over my shoulder to the jumpmaster. Uncertainty disappeared in an instant: his boot was poised to kick me out the door. I jumped, grabbed the handle to my reserve 'chute, and counted to three.

I felt the thrilling tug of the air on my chute and looked up to check the canopy. It was perfect: smooth and round, no rips or snapped risers—a thing of glory, God-like in its lifesaving power. And I felt more alive than at any other time of my life.

## Epilogue

One of the most thrilling things about military parachuting is the instant transition from the chaos of wind, sound and vibration to a quiet, smooth drift in the sky with a privileged view of the countryside. It offers an interlude of solitude unlike any other. I have experienced something like it only in one other setting: plunging into the weightless serenity of the sea from the lurching, noisome deck of a scuba-diving boat.

✲ ✲ ✲

I've had a lot of schooling in my day, and though only three weeks long, I rank jump school as one of my better educational experiences.

I loved being in the 101st Airborne Division, the fabled group from D-Day. During my two-year tour I developed great respect for and admiration of the US military. I came close to making it a career. Despite the brevity of my service, I came to appreciate the bond that exists among members of the military, which stays with us for a lifetime. It is, as Shakespeare put it, a "band of brothers." There is no way to be brother but to serve.

CHAPTER 9

# Paratrooper Circumcision

## Prologue

After completing jump school I was assigned to the 101st Airborne Division, headquartered at Fort Campbell, Kentucky, in a rural area on the Tennessee border.

O h, Doc!" was the last thing he said before fainting. It was the last straw, a bizarrely fitting climax to a minor surgical procedure. That is, if any surgery on the penis can be considered minor.

I don't remember what I said when his considerable bulk collapsed on my surgical handiwork, but it must have been "Oh, shit!" or the equivalent.

His temporarily insensate state reinforced a conviction that had been growing in the course of a muggy, late spring afternoon. If I ever get him and me out of this mess, I am never going to do anything so stupid again. This sensible conclusion was followed by an equally certain resolve. I was not cut out to be a surgeon.

I had nobody to blame but myself. Eighteen months earlier I had been a General Medical Officer stationed in the Pentagon. It was an easy, clean, air-conditioned job. Despite the fact that my duties there were responsible for three of the most interesting days of my life as a participant in the JFK funeral, the work was boring, I had to wear the Army equivalent of a banker's suit, and I hated riding the bus to work. Volunteering to be a military parachutist was my ticket out.

After qualifying as a parachutist, I was assigned as Battalion Surgeon for the 501st Parachute Infantry Regiment of the famed "Screaming Eagles" of the 101st Airborne Division, the intrepid unit that parachuted inland from the Normandy beaches in advance of the main D-Day assault forces, and who later became known as the "Battered Bastards of Bastogne" in the Battle of the Bulge at Christmas 1944.

It was heady stuff. "Battalion Surgeon" had a nice ring to it, despite the fact that my experience with actual surgery was as a medical student, and pretty much limited to holding retractors in an abdominal incision while real surgeons did the work. The title, however, added to a certain bulletproof feeling, natural to twenty-seven-year-old males, but armor-plated in me after saving lives as an intern and jumping out of perfectly good airplanes and living to tell of it.

I reigned over a kingdom of about a dozen Army medics, most of them not long out of high school. It was wonderful. They were sculpted to conform absolutely to military discipline and drilled in the doctrine of instant obedience to authority. And I was vested with authority—new to a former lowly medical student and intern—which conveyed a feeling of power and mastery that I found pleasing. Very pleasing. Soon I came to believe I was actually masterful and powerful.

My word was law, in certain circumstances practically above that of the commanding officer. Most COs didn't want to cross "the doc" and mine, a tired veteran of the Korean War, was no exception. We regularly traded favors. On winter bivouacs I would slip him a quart of "medicinal" scotch and he'd give me extra gasoline for the heater in the aid station tent, where I tenderly cared for the many malingerers who wanted in out of the cold.

It was in this state of mind that I agreed to become team doctor for the 101st Airborne Division football team, where I found the same reverence for "the doc." Having played football in high school, I got pumped up in anticipation of each game and eager to do my part to ensure victory.

Not being one who would break the ancient and mystical traditions surrounding my calling, I continued the practice of my predecessor shaman in the temple of paratrooper football by administering magical potions. In one ritual I stood at the door and, as the gladiators passed out to battle, popped little white pills into their open gullets like a mother bird tending her chicks. Already fully charged with testosterone, they bolted onto the field further stoked by amphetamines. And when violence tore at their bodies and they hobbled to the sideline, I was there for them, ready with crystalline phials of powerful liquids, which I injected to numb the injury or to cloud the pain in a gauzy haze of morphine. "The doc" could do no wrong.

It was against this background of adulation that our quarterback, the starting quarterback at West Point a few years before, asked me to circumcise him before his wedding. Ordinarily this would have been a task for a urologist. One was at the post hospital, but he was a notorious drunk, so the quarterback asked me. We were brothers at arms, and after all, I had an M.D. degree, I had survived the hell of paratrooper school, and had about a dozen jumps under my belt. I could conquer the world, especially the dull and simple art of surgery of the penis.

He pleaded that he was getting married, and "I know you can do it." It was all the encouragement I needed. We agreed that it was safer for me to do it in the battalion aid station than to trust his vital equipment to unsteady hands in the urology department at the hospital. After all, how many men can say they have been circumcised by a paratrooper.

I reassured him, and myself, that I'd done a few before. This bordered on an outright lie. I'd done a few infant circumcisions, a task so easy that medical students were routinely given the job because it relied on a simple mechanical device that basically pinched off the collar of skin and required no stitches. However, I had seen an adult circumcision in urology clinic and the task was in perfect accord with the mantra we heard as medical students: "See one, do one, teach one." I'm still waiting for my teaching opportunity.

However, not wanting to trust entirely to experience, I visited the library at the post hospital. Unfortunately no surgical textbook was on hand, so I settled on an anatomy text to remind myself about the nerves and blood supply. The text clearly demonstrated the bountiful supply of each.

The day of the great event was hot, muggy and windless. We assembled shortly after noon in a tiny room in the battalion aid station. The patient was sweating profusely and had a big belly, proving the maxim enunciated later by Washington Redskin quarterback Sonny Jergensen, who responded to criticism of his famous beer belly: "I don't throw the ball with my stomach."

I gave him a horse-size dose of morphine to ensure docility and dreamy compliance with my instructions, and ordered him to strip naked and lie on his back on the table where his organ would be readily available to my ministrations. I wish I could say that the object of our attention was a weapon which made men stare and women cringe, but it was quite ordinary, clad as it was with a modest collar of foreskin, which I confidently and loudly bragged would be shorn away in short order. I tugged it aloft and invited my corpsmen to inspect the anatomy and gave a short lecture on exactly what was to occur.

As the morphine took hold, our victim made nervous jokes with my assistants while I drew up a syringe of Novocaine and capped it with a long needle, the better to reach some of the deeper nerves in the groin, which required accurate injection to deaden the penis. He moaned and squirmed for a while, but after the first few injections he became quiet again.

A circumcision is really quite simple. The collar of foreskin is pulled forward and two cuts are made, both in line with the middle of the shaft, one on the top and one on the bottom of the foreskin. This creates two lateral skin flaps, one attached to either side of the penis at the base of the head. These are trimmed away close to the shaft and the resulting circumferential wound is sutured. And, voila, the deed is done!

One of the tricks of this procedure is to use a special long, thin clamp, somewhat like "hog-nose" pliers, to crush the tissue where the initial top and bottom cuts are to be made. This crushing welds the tissue together so that the cuts can be made in the impression left by the clamp. Having crushed the blood vessels and nerves, no bleeding or pain accompanies the initial cuts. However, when I applied the clamp, my patient, whom I'd forgotten remained attached to his penis, groaned loudly and in his stupor began groping to remove the offending stimulus.

I quickly released the clamp and ordered the corpsmen to tie his arms to the table. After he was suitably bound, I drew up more anesthetic, and injected a full syringe, jabbing here and there at the unseen nerves that had been so easily identifiable in the textbook. By the time I finished, his groin was lumpy and swollen with what amounted to a figurative barrel of Novocaine. Again the clamp produced groans and thrashing. I relaxed the clamp and ordered a chest strap be added to the restraints.

By this time I was sweating, nervous and tired, and envious of my patient who, after the offending clamp was removed, lay in peaceful repose. I eyed my work. It did not inspire confidence. His organ issued from a mound of tortured flesh—lumpy, hairy, and oozing blood from the many injection sites, and looking much like he'd gotten in a barroom fight using his organ against an opponent armed with a baseball bat.

But this was no time for second thoughts or half measures, so I applied the clamp with extra vigor and held on until the thrashing stopped.

Next I made the top and bottom incisions and to my delight the tissue parted cleanly and without further protest or bleeding.  But by now a fifteen minute surgery had lasted for the better part of two hours and the morphine was wearing off.  Our patient raised his head, straining against his fetters, looked glassily down toward me and said, "Doc, I changed my mind."

I dispatched him with more morphine and returned to my labors.  My next task was to trim off the flaps by cutting across the base of each one close to the shaft of the penis.  It proved far more difficult than anticipated.  It was hard to tell where the flap ended and the penis began.  I was all very loose and flabby.  So I cut a bit here and a bit there, extending my cuts around the edge of the shaft until we got to that most sensitive part on the bottom side of the shaft near the tip.

Each time I made a small cut the groaning and thrashing began anew.  So, I drew up one last syringe of Novocaine and injected more.  But to no avail.  Every time I tried to trim across the last bit of foreskin he screeched drunken objections.

By this time I was issuing silent promises to heaven that if I was delivered from this situation I would forever keep my promise never to sneer at surgeons as mere mechanics.  In this desperate condition I decided I would deaden the recalcitrant zone with a direct injection.  I drew yet another syringe of Novocaine and stuck it into the end of his penis.  Our patient bucked and groaned, and the loose tissue swelled with frightening distortion, its lonely eye now askew with a doubtful glance above a drooping, bloody collar.

I cut again. More thrashing and groaning. Another injection, more cuts, louder groans. By now at wits end I experienced the truth of a maxim oft repeated in medical school, usually in the emergency room over the near lifeless form of a victim of The Saturday Night Knife and Gun Club: *Desperate conditions call for desperate measures.*

In a moment of resolve unforgettable at the distance of forty years, I said to myself: Enough is enough. I grabbed a pair of scissors, pulled forward tightly on the two recalcitrant pieces of tissue, took approximate aim and, in a swoop worthy of an executioner in the court of Henry VIII, I chopped. Screams! Success!

Now to the suturing. I had assumed that the operating room would have an ample supply of sutures. I was right, but the stiff, heavy stuff was more suited to closing shrapnel wounds than the delicate task at hand. I began to stitch, but the damned things were so stiff they wouldn't stay tied with an ordinary square knot. So I tied a string of knots in each, a technique more akin to plaiting cornrows in a hair salon than surgical suturing. The result bristled wildly like a rapper's dreadlocks.

Next came the bandaging. Like most other parts of this ill-advised undertaking I assumed it would bandage it like anything else—but it was more akin to bandaging a piece of spaghetti. I wrapped this way and that, careful to leave a peep-hole. None of the successive wraps produced the desired result; the bandage seemed ready to slide away at any moment. I added more and more until I had swathed the thing into a satisfying mound that was secured to his belly by big swaths of white tape.

I roused our patient from his slumber and asked him to stand and lean against the side of the table. My purpose was to see if the bandage, or his penis, would fall off. He wavered there, grinning foolishly and then looked down to see what had been wrought. A single drop of blood plopped to the floor between his feet. He looked back up at me with a vacant stare and said, "Oh, Doc," and fell over in a faint, crushing my work.

We revived him in short order, due no doubt to a favorable Heavenly response to the most fervent prayers ever issued by a circumciser. I ordered my corpsmen to get him dressed while I went outside to gasp for fresh air. Shortly one of my assistants came to explain that they had an unusual problem: they couldn't get his penis back in his pants. The thing and its bandage were too large. Our patient, by now hurting and belligerent, wasn't going to leave the aid station with his organ hanging out of his pants.

I confronted him and gave him a military order that he would damn well do as I instructed. Just when I was about to send him out into world with his surgery showing, one of my corpsmen suggested we cover him with a poncho. So we pulled up his pants, leaving his organ protruding, buckled his belt, draped a poncho over him and sent him home. A few days later I saw him at the PX, blithely going down the aisles in his poncho.

My last instruction to him was about how to avoid an erection, improbable to be sure, but one which could have torn out the sutures. I gave him a bottle of the compressed "freezing gas" used by my football assistants to spray sprained ankles and knees, and instructed him to give his penis an icy blast should hormones prove mightier than the knife.

I saw him for the final time when he came back for his last post-op visit. The result was noteworthy for what some might call a rakish slant, but in my part of the South we call it catawampus. It was enough to make men cringe and women stare. He was happy with the result.

# CHAPTER 10

# A Woman Scorned

**Prologue**

I completed my two year military obligation in July 1965 and returned to Parkland Hospital for four years of pathology training. Pay was poor and I had a family to support, so I took a night call job weekends in a small suburban clinic.

The clinic door buzzer jarred me awake. I looked at the clock: 1 AM. It was ample validation of my decision to become a pathologist, a specialty medical tribe who, in my rosy imaginings, were never disturbed by anything more than the hum of computers and the gentle clack of lab instruments. But I wasn't a pathologist; not yet, anyway. I was a lowly first year pathology trainee making a meager stipend with four years of serfdom ahead, and I was taking night call at a clinic to support a wife and child. Tonight was my first night at a small medical clinic, and it had gone well: just a few patients, each of whom had a minor problem that was easy to manage.

I shuffled to the door. My visitor was a young woman with an infant in her arms. "She's been crying all day and I just couldn't wait until morning for a doctor to see her," she said, nervous as only new mothers can be.

It was just the three of us in the middle of the night in an otherwise empty clinic. It was a far cry from my medical student and intern days, where I had been just a cog in a larger wheel with ready access to x-rays, lab tests, and experienced physicians. Now I was on my own. Feeling more than a bit apprehensive, I guided her to the exam room.

Following the pediatric aphorism, "Listen to the mother and she will tell you the diagnosis," I asked the usual questions, all the while studying the infant, a four-month-old girl who was a patient of the pediatrician at the clinic. She was a first child, the healthy product of a normal pregnancy and had the usual immunizations. She had been cranky for couple of days with a mild fever and messy nose. Tonight her temperature had risen a bit higher than before. The mother volunteered, "She just couldn't go to sleep, so I decided to bring her in." I asked about seizures, rashes, wheezes, difficulty breathing, diarrhea, and so on. Nothing unusual surfaced, and I concluded she had an ordinary upper respiratory virus infection and would be fine in a day or two. But before reaching final conclusions, I needed to examine her.

We laid her out on an exam table and I inserted a rectal thermometer while mother held her still. The baby had a mild fever; nothing alarming. She looked perfectly healthy: pink, no rash, with fat little cheeks and thighs, a robust cry, and mucus crusted around her nostrils. Heart and respiratory rate were rapid, but in the expected range for a feverish infant.

Meningitis was foremost in my mind as something to rule out. My first born, Anne, then two, had meningitis a few months earlier and might have died had I not recognized subtle signs and taken her to the hospital quickly. I felt the soft spot in the baby's skull. It was reassuringly soft and flat, not tense and bulging as it would have been with meningitis. Her neck was flexible and she didn't cry when I twisted her head from side to side as she would have done if she had meningitis. She wasn't lethargic, nor was she jumpy, the two things that had combined in Anne to alert me that there was more to her fever than the infected ear the pediatrician had diagnosed the day before.

I looked in the baby's ears. The drums were flat, shiny and pearly—nothing there of the dull, red bulge of infection. Finally, I put a stethoscope to her chest, a few mucus rattles, but no asthmatic wheezes, and her heart sounds were normal. In short, it was the typical history and exam findings for the usual type of non-threatening viral respiratory infection that occur regularly in every child.

Then I made a mistake. Trying to admit that no doctor could know which of the many possible viruses afflicted her infant, I said, "I don't know exactly what is wrong with your baby, but I can assure you it's not anything serious. She doesn't have an ear infection, meningitis, or pneumonia. She's probably got a virus infection and she'll be over it in a day or two. You can give her baby aspirin and sponge baths for the fever."

This is not what a new mother wants to hear. "Probably! Probably is not good enough. You don't know what's wrong with her, do you!" she said, beginning to sob.

"That's not correct, I . . ." She cut me off.

"You just said you didn't know," she wailed. "No, wonder. You haven't done any lab tests or X-rays."

I explained that the clinic lab and X-ray were closed. I was the only person at the clinic and didn't know how to operate the equipment, a statement that made me seem lame.

"My baby is sick and needs penicillin. Give her a shot of penicillin. What are you waiting for? And I want a prescription," she demanded.

All the while the child was screaming. Exasperated, I launched into an explanation of what I had done to ensure nothing serious threatened her child. "Penicillin nor any other antibiotic is going to help your baby, ma'am," I concluded, "penicillin doesn't kill viruses, just bacteria, and your baby doesn't have a bacterial infection."

"You don't know that for sure. Call a doctor!" she demanded. I wanted to say, "I *am* a doctor," but thought better of it.

"I am not going to wake up your doctor at 1 AM about a baby with a mild fever and a runny nose," I said. "And besides," I lectured, "there's a danger that treating virus infections with penicillin just makes babies immune to the effect of penicillin. There's a good chance we'd just be encouraging the growth of super-germs that penicillin can't kill. If something truly serious comes along in the future that's one less antibiotic we could use to save her life. " And just to ram the point home, I jabbed her with the professional secret of such matters: "Giving this baby prescription medicines is nothing more than an elaborate form of psychotherapy—*for you!*"

This is a true saying and worthy to be received by all males: Hell hath no fury like a woman scorned. As she ranted, all I could think of to say was "No, I will not call the doctor; No, I will not give her a shot of penicillin; No, I will not write a prescription; Your baby is going to be fine. Just rely on aspirin and sponge baths." After more sobbing and shouting she left in a rage, threatening as she walked out the door to have my job, and to sue for malpractice.

I was so tense and upset I couldn't get back to sleep. Never before had I had such a sour encounter with a patient. It didn't take much thought to conclude that I would have been much wiser to administer the psychotherapy required. Make up name for the baby's illness. Something like "multiple idiopathic hickyosis" would have done the trick. And I should have written a prescription for some innocuous something.

As I lay there, a great truth dawned on me. There are two grand imperatives in medicine: NAME the disease, and DO something. Anything. Physical examinations, careful questioning, considered judgment and reassurance usually don't count. Injections, lab tests, X-rays, and prescriptions are much better.

### Epilogue

During the course of this opera I suppressed an urge to ask, as I often had as a medical student and intern, "Why are you here at 1 AM instead of 8 PM?" I would have liked to know, but she was angry enough already. The answers were usually interesting. The most memorable, provided several years earlier in the University of Mississippi emergency room at 3 AM by another mother with a crying infant: "My husband drives a milk truck and he gave me a ride."

Worried that my angry patient would make more trouble, the next day I called the pediatrician to alert him. He didn't return my call for a few days, but when we talked he told me that he'd seen the baby and she was fine. With a chuckle he told me I'd done exactly the right thing medically, but I had a few things to learn about patient relations.

CHAPTER 11

# Autopsies, Bullets, and the JFK Assassination

## Prologue

In addition to night and weekend clinic work, I did some medicolegal (forensic) autopsies for the Dallas Medical Examiner's office. Like most pathology residents, I needed the money and took my turn when the lone forensic pathologist was on vacation, testifying, or otherwise not available. The cases we were assigned to do were usually simple: gunshots, stabbings, car wrecks and other mayhem.

The word *autopsy* derives from Greek *autos* = self and *optos* = seen; that is, to see for one's self. About 3000 BC, in their practice of mummification, Egyptians became the first to leave a historical record of socially approved invasion of the body after death.

Records from the first century AD reveal that a few curious Roman and Greek intellectuals dissected bodies in their investigations of anatomy. From then until the Renaissance only a few reports of human dissection were recorded. Dissection in the name of science gradually regained social acceptance beginning in the 16th century.

Nowadays pathologists do most autopsies. It is widely and erroneously believed that most autopsies are done to determine the cause of death. Actually, modern diagnostic techniques are so good that in most instances the cause of death is clear, it's details that are missing.

During my time as a resident hospitals were required to obtain autopsies in a certain percentage of deaths in order to retain their eligibility to receive Medicare payments and to maintain official accreditation. Autopsy rates were high, in some institutions surpassing 50%. The autopsy requirement was eliminated in 1971. Nowadays autopsies are done on less than 5% of patients dying in hospitals, sometimes much less.

The situation is different in autopsies done for legal purposes. Sometimes a person dies unobserved, in suspicious circumstances, from violence, or in certain other circumstances and the law requires an investigation. Many times the cause of death may be clear, but an autopsy will be ordered to accumulate evidence.

In the investigation of gunshot wounds one of the most important things done at autopsy is to map the course of the bullet from entry to exit and to recover the bullet if it is still in the body.

Nowadays specially trained (forensic) pathologists perform these autopsies in the course of their duty as official medical examiners. But it was far different in the 1960s when I was in general pathology training at Parkland Hospital. Back then Dallas had but a single forensic pathologist, Earl Rose, who was greatly overworked and underpaid. The "Saturday night knife and gun club," as we called it, provided a steady stream of corpses, sometimes a half-dozen or so per day. All had to be autopsied, wounds precisely described, bullets retrieved, and so on. If Earl wasn't around the residents were eager to do them for the $35 fee. And we were especially eager for gunshot victims because the task was usually so straightforward. But if a "floater" came along, a decomposing body fetched from the Trinity River, for example, and it was your turn, you were stuck.

One of the first tricks I learned about gunshot autopsies with no exit wound was to feel for the bullet beneath the skin at a point directly opposite the entry wound. This owes to the fact that skin is the toughest thing a bullet has to penetrate. Think about it. Skin is, quite literally, tough as leather, bullets do not have a sharp tip, and they are generally made of lead and brass, relatively soft metals. Passing through skin sucks a lot of energy out of a bullet, which spends further energy crashing through internal organs or bone before finally trying to fist its way through skin on the other side. Sometimes it runs out of gas and the second layer of skin catches it like a ball in a net. Sometimes all I had to do was run my hand over the skin, feeling for the telltale lump, nick the skin and pull it out. Easy pickings.

Other times bullets were hard to find. They hid in muscle, bone and other tissues, the task of finding them confounded by gouts of clotted blood. Sometimes we'd know we were close but just couldn't find it, so we'd put a metal marker on the spot and call radiology to take an x-ray. On most occasions the bullet was fractions of an inch away.

One such experience came in the case of a man shot multiple times with small caliber (.22) bullets. He had lived a short while in the hospital. I easily found all but one of the bullets. The missing one vanished after passing through the front chest wall and the aorta, the big artery that distributes blood from the heart to every other artery in the body. There was no exit wound on the man's back, so the bullet had to be in there somewhere.

It was frustrating. Blood obscured and distorted the anatomy. I poked here and cut there, but try as I might, I could not find the bullet. I called radiology and asked them to roll a portable x-ray machine to the morgue to take a picture of the corpse's chest. They did, but no bullet was visible. I asked for a second picture lower down.

This did not sit well with the x-ray tech, an old-timer who clearly did not relish being in the morgue. No one but a pathologist feels at home in an autopsy suite. Most people, including other professionals, want to get out as quickly as they can. What's more, taking a postmortem x-ray involves maneuvering the corpse to insert a film cassette beneath. It is a cumbersome, sloppy task that requires a lot of effort. Now I was asking the tech to take a second x-ray. It was clear he thought I needed his help to make up for my lack of skill, a conclusion surely reinforced when no bullet showed up in the second picture.

Then it dawned on me that maybe the bullet had gone into the aorta but didn't have enough energy to exit, and could have traveled downward with the flow of blood. I made the mistake of explaining this rationale to the tech. He brusquely pointed out that the body had so many bullet holes that maybe I had mixed up entrance and exit wounds and there was no bullet to be found because it had exited through one of the many holes. But to his credit he agreed to another picture and we shot one of the pelvis. Nothing.

I asked him for one more shot, this one of the thighs and knees. He agreed. And with that we found it. There it was, in the hollow of the left knee. It had been swept downstream in the river of aortic blood and stopped when it got to a tributary in the knee too small for it to travel further.

Improbable as the behavior of that bullet was, it was not the oddest. I had two other unusual gunshot cases, which inform my opinion about the Kennedy assassination and the Warren Report (Chapter 21).

In each instance the patient was dead on arrival and the corpse was rolled into the morgue in street clothes. Morgue attendants were trained to inventory personal items such as rings and watches, clothing, and so on. In each of these cases the attendant found a bullet loose in the clothing. In one case it was loose beneath a thin cotton T-shirt, after fisting its way through the skin of the back, tearing through heart and lungs with fatal effect, and burrowing through the skin of the front of the chest, all without having enough residual energy to tear through the flimsy material of a T-shirt. The evidence was plain: a bullet hole in the back of the T-shirt, in the skin of the back and in the skin of the chest, but no exit hole in the front of the T-shirt.

That I saw two such cases in doing a few gunshot autopsies suggests that it must be more common than ordinarily imagined.

✳ ✳ ✳

Which brings me to the Kennedy assassination. I believe Oswald was the only shooter. I have many reasons for believing so. For example, I have been shooting bolt-action, high-powered rifles all of my life. I have stood in that window on the sixth floor of the former Texas School Book Depository, and looked down on Dealy Plaza and Elm Street. I could have made those shots easily. This is not the place to debate conspiracy theories about a second gunman, but I do offer an alternative explanation for which shot did which injuries to whom. I find my explanation more reasonable than the Warren Commission findings, which might convince a few skeptics, but I'm not holding my breath.

The Warren Commission (and almost everyone else) believed, as do I, that the third and last bullet hit Kennedy in the head. The Warren Commission also held that Kennedy and Connally were hit by a single bullet (the famed Single Bullet Theory), either from the first or the second shot. This requires that one shot miss the entire limousine. This seems unlikely. It was a big, slow-moving target. It also requires that the single bullet tear through two layers of skin in Kennedy's neck and his clothing, two layers of skin on Connally's chest plus a rib and his clothing, two layers of skin and a bone in his arm, and a final layer of skin and clothing on his thigh. This makes seven layers of skin and clothing plus two bones and assorted other flesh.

Jump now to Parkland Hospital where a bullet from Oswald's rifle was found on a gurney. Which gurney is not certain, Kennedy's or Connally's. This bullet was in nearly pristine condition. The Warren Commission held that this bullet inflicted the neck wounds on Kennedy and all of the wounds on Connally. For several reasons this seems unlikely to me and to many others, most of whom are conspiracy theorists.

First, for the Single Bullet Theory to explain the evidence it seems to require that the bullet take a zig-zag course through the two men. I have no opinion on that point.

Second, what I find unlikely is that the Pristine Bullet could have passed through seven layers of skin and clothing and two bones and be no more deformed than it was.

Finally, add John Connally's insistence that the first bullet did not hit him. He grew up in Texas using high-powered rifles and knew the sound. He insisted, and I believe him, that at the sound of the first shot he turned to his right to see where the shot came from and was not hit until he turned back to his left to look for Kennedy.

I offer the following scenario, which seems to fit better with much of the other evidence than the Single Bullet Theory. It does not require a missed shot at a very big target, the limousine. It does not require that one nearly perfectly formed bullet do so much damage to skin, bone and flesh, and it does not require a zig-zag bullet path.

My thesis is this. The first shot hit Kennedy in the neck, traveled through his neck and exited through the front of his neck but did not have enough energy to escape his clothing. This must be the Pristine Bullet found on the gurney. Connally was hit by the second shot, the fragments of which ended their flight buried in his thigh. He carried this opinion and the bullet fragments to his grave. The third, fatal, bullet hit Kennedy in the head.

CHAPTER 12

# Last Gasp

**Prologue**

I finished my residency in 1969 and began private practice in a small suburban hospital.

**I answered the phone.** "Doctor McConnell?" the voice inquired.

"Yes," I said.

It was a staff physician. "Could you come up to the operating room?" he said. "I have a situation to discuss with you."

Most of the time a pathologist is summoned to the operating room it is to perform a quick microscopic diagnosis on a scrap of tissue to see if it is malignant; something like a breast biopsy, for example. If the pathologist finds it to be malignant, cancer surgery is performed. If the verdict is benign, the wound is closed and that's the end of it. But the doctor was an Ob-Gyn, not the type ordinarily in need of an operating room visit by a pathologist. Maybe it was a lab goof-up on a blood or urine specimen from one of his patients and he was summoning me, the laboratory director, to complain.

I grabbed a copy of the operating room schedule and scanned it, trying to get an idea about what might be up, but the doctor had no cases posted. Furthermore, it was the middle of the afternoon and the daily surgery schedule had finished hours earlier. It was puzzling and a little unsettling. Maybe it was the tone of his voice or his use of the word "situation" that set me on edge.

I found him in the doctors' lounge in the otherwise empty operating rooms.

"Thank you for coming," he said. "I've got a really touchy issue on my hands and I need your advice." He told me of a young pregnant woman near term that he'd admitted to the hospital earlier in the day. The pregnancy had been normal at first but in the last couple of months her uterus had grown much too large. Ultrasound diagnosis was unknown in those days so he had been compelled get an x-ray image to see what was happening.

"The instant I saw those films I knew there was going to be trouble," he said. The x-rays showed that the baby had a huge head filled with fluid and almost no brain.

"It's hydrocephalus of the worst kind," he said. "She'll never deliver normally, the head's way too big. And I can't bring myself to do a Caesarian section on her just to retrieve an infant that will never draw a breath. She will need a general anesthetic and with a case this unusual I worry that something strange could happen. If anything happened to her I'd never be able to live with myself for having opted to do a C-section when I could do something safer. This is her first pregnancy, and if she has a C-section and she has more kids she'll have to have every one by C-section," he continued, referring to the standard practice. "But there is an alternative and that's what I want to talk to you about."

As he was telling me this story I kept asking myself: What does this have to do with pathology? Then it occurred to me that maybe he was testing his idea with someone he who could offer disinterested advice.

He then told me of an instrument that had rested unused for years on an operating room storage shelf. I later saw it—a stainless steel contraption with three long, toothed tongs that could be closed around the fetus's skull. In the center was a corkscrew-like device for drilling a hole in the skull to release the fluid, after which the tongs could be used to crush the skull and pull the fetus through the birth canal. This would avoid the necessity for a C-section.

He said, "Of necessity, this is going to be an all-physician undertaking. The nurses have gotten wind of it and none of them will help. It's a very tense situation. What I need from you is an autopsy that will document the hydrocephalus and anything else you find. And I'll need you in the delivery room to take the baby and carry it to the morgue yourself. I doubt any hospital staff will do it. Even if they would do it, I wouldn't allow it. We might find a picture on the front page tomorrow. I've gone over all of this with the mother and father and they are very distressed, but agreeable. So, what do you think? Am I crazy?"

I told him I thought his plan was a good one and I would perform the autopsy.

So the deed was done. True to the doctor's prediction, the infant never took a breath. I wrapped it in a heavy white cotton surgical drape and took the back stairs down to the basement, where the morgue was located at the end of a long, poorly lit hall, the door illuminated by a bare bulb. With every step my mission seemed more and more like a B-grade horror movie.

I locked the door with the dead bolt and, thankful to be alone, opened my sad little package and placed the tiny corpse on the big stainless steel autopsy table. After a short time I was gowned and gloved and had the instruments and dictation apparatus ready. I dictated the usual opening, introducing myself, the date, time and place and the assigned autopsy number. It was about 30 minutes after the birth.

Almost every autopsy incision is a large Y-shaped cut. Each arm of the Y begins on the front of each shoulder and extends down to the lower end of the chest, where they join and extend to the lower end of the abdomen. As I held the knife above the little form I took one last look at its face. It was small and angular, not at all the round face of a healthy infant, and dwarfed by the huge, high forehead. I made a mental note to describe the pinched facial appearance, which is sometimes a clue to serious internal congenital abnormalities.

I heaved a sigh. It's impossible to maintain emotional detachment, especially standing over a dead child. I placed the knife on the right shoulder and drew it downward. As it crossed the chest the infant gasped. My heart nearly stopped. In an instant I knew what had happened. I'd inadvertently cut into the chest cavity and triggered the collapse of the right lung, which in turn activated a well-known and powerful reflex that operates to expand the chest when lung volume is too low. It is one of thousands of protective reflexes, each of which operate to maintain normal body function. Such reflexes operate through the deepest, most primitive or "reptilian" brain, far below consciousness. At least a few cells in the child's nubbin of brain were still alive to relay the nerve impulses and a few chest muscles were also alive to carry out the command. Every other cell in the body may have been dead—no heartbeat or other motion—but a flicker of life still burned in a few places.

Never was I more grateful for solitude. Explaining to anyone other than another physician would have been impossible. Besides, what was I to do, call the crash cart from the intensive care unit?

I stood frozen in the moment. The body remained perfectly still—no other respiratory effort. No sound but my own breathing and the hum of a motor somewhere.

So I turned again to the task, worried a bit that a small part of the heart might be quivering ineffectively, as I'd seen once before in an autopsy on an adult. To my relief nothing else unusual occurred. In addition to the hydrocephalus I found a serious congenital heart defect and almost total lack of brain tissue.

### Epilogue

Take from this story what you will. Life presents difficult choices. In the debate about abortion I come down on the side of a woman's right to choose.

# CHAPTER 13

# Phos-fate

**Prologue**

This episode also occurred in the small suburban hospital where I was in private practice after finishing my pathology training.

It promised to be another long day at the microscope looking at biopsies and pap smears, so an interruption wasn't unwelcome. I needed a break.

"Look at this, Dr. McConnell," the lab tech said, holding up a rack of test tubes containing purple fluid.

"This is today's run of blood phosphates. Something is not right about this one," she continued, pointing to a tube so purple it was nearly black. The remaining ones from other patients were varying shades of much paler purple, reflecting minor differences of blood phosphate from one patient to another. "I've done this one three times and it always comes out near forty-five. This patient is in the emergency room and she's in critical condition."

She and I knew that normal blood phosphate was usually about four, not forty. No medical condition could explain that number. The level of blood phosphate doesn't vary much in healthy people. At most, even under the most extreme conditions—kidney failure, for example—it might rise to eight or ten. But forty-five? Impossible. It had to be an error, maybe soap contamination in the specimen or test tubes—some soaps contain a lot of phosphate.

Puzzling over shades of purple is not what the public imagines pathologists do. By their reckoning all of our energy is devoted to the dark work of carving up the dead in dim hospital basements. It has always been a sore point for me. Actually most of us spend as much time sorting through lab test reports, or consulting with other doctors as we do looking through a microscope. Autopsies occupy only a small fraction of our time.

This kind of laboratory oddity, a seemingly outrageous test result, was right up my alley. From the very beginning of my training to be a pathologist I found that lab testing—the science of the test procedure, quality control, instrumentation, interpretation of the result, and every other aspect—appealed to me more than autopsies and microscopic work.

Sorting out this mystery might even be fun. I had been in practice only slightly over a year, so I was eager to make my mark, but I hadn't yet come across a situation where a single odd laboratory result unlocked a mystery. Maybe this was it.

Most outrageous results turn out to be mistakes or due to specimen contamination or something else that has nothing to do with what is actually happening in the patient's body. The workings of the body demand that substances in blood stay in a narrow range, so this had to be something other than a true representation of the patient's condition. I told the tech to go back to the beginning and start anew: collect a fresh blood specimen from the patient and redo the test using fresh reagents and new, freshly washed and dried tubes, no soap allowed.

I returned to my slides and in about a half an hour she was back with the same result. Despite the apparent lack of laboratory error, I couldn't bring myself to authorize release of such a preposterous result without further investigation. If it was an error, as it surely must be, I would look foolish at least—careers are derailed over such things and I was just getting started. I asked her to collect all of the lab results we had on the patient and get back to me quickly.

I sorted through the stack of lab reports. The patient was mildly anemic, her kidney numbers suggested a problem there, her fluid balance numbers weren't quite right, and some of her other values were somewhat out of whack, but no pattern emerged. Then I saw that her blood calcium was five—half of what it should have been—a result as wildly improbable as the phosphate. Calcium is among the most tightly regulated substances in blood, and I'd never seen one anywhere near this low. But despite the absurd values for each, the combination made a certain amount of sense: blood phosphorous and calcium vary inversely, and her preposterously high phosphate was appropriately matched by nonsensically low calcium. I felt like a detective with a fresh clue in a murder case but no suspect in sight. There had to be an answer; there always was. The trick was to find it. I needed more information.

I weighed what to do next. The patient and her chart were in the ER, just one floor down. A trip to the ER seemed in order, but I was nervous about the prospect. I was new to the hospital, I didn't know the doctors well, and I wasn't sure I would be welcome. An uninvited doctor, especially a pathologist, nosing around with someone else's patient might not sit well.

In the ER I found her doctor. This was before emergency specialists staffed emergency rooms and the doctor had been called away from his busy office. I introduced myself and held up the rack of purple tubes as my excuse for butting in. To my relief he welcomed my interest. He'd already done a physical exam and some x-rays and was glad to have the laboratory results.

The patient was a forty-eight year-old, very obese woman who had had a seizure at home and failed to regain consciousness. Her blood pressure was low, her breathing fast and shallow, and her heartbeat was fast, with lots of irregular, crazy beats. Her medical history was sketchy. She lived alone and it wasn't clear who had brought her to the hospital. In any case, they were gone.

She was semicomatose and still. I pressed a knuckle hard into her chest to check her response to pain. She groaned slightly but didn't move. She seemed to be paralyzed, an observation that jived with her blood calcium: muscles require calcium to do their work of moving the body, and apparently her blood wasn't supplying enough. Low calcium would also explain the crazy heartbeats. The heart is a muscle and it, too, was starving for calcium. A picture was beginning to form.

The other notable thing was her belly, which was huge and filled with fluid. There are hundreds of conditions that cause fluid to accumulate in the belly, so many that finding fluid didn't offer much help. I took a stethoscope and listened to her belly. It was ominously quiet. When the bowels are working properly intestinal fluids and gas slosh around, making tinkling and gurgling sounds. The low calcium must have paralyzed her intestines, too.

I had a good discussion with her doctor. We agreed about the effect of the profoundly low calcium. It explained everything, including the seizure and coma. But neither of us could account for the phosphate. He had called a surgeon to evaluate her intestinal problem and a cardiologist for her irregular heartbeat. There was nothing else for me to do, so I retreated to the lab without an answer to the problem. Even so, I felt a surge of confidence because I had been welcomed as a member of a team working on a critically ill patient.

Later in the day I got a call from the ER. The patient had died from a cardiac arrest, not a surprise given the wild behavior of her heartbeats in the hours before death. Would I do an autopsy if permission could be obtained from the family, or if an order could be obtained from the local Justice of the Peace?*

I have never liked doing autopsies. It is a point of pride among pathologists that autopsies are valuable investigations that often turn up surprises despite modern diagnostic techniques that seem to reveal everything possible about human anatomy and physiology. But it is a rare pathologist who likes doing them. On the surface it is smelly, bloody, greasy work, but on a deeper level it is an intimate confrontation with your own mortality.

The patient's obesity—a curse in death as in life— made the autopsy messier and more difficult than most. When I cut into her abdomen an odious rush of liquid feces spilled from the incision. Grimacing behind my mask, which did nothing to filter out the odor, I scooped out most of it and poked around, looking for her abdominal organs, but they were nowhere to be seen. After clearing away more feces it became evident that I was inside her colon, ordinarily a soft muscular tube a bit smaller than a wrist. Hers, however, was massively dilated—ballooned with a stupefying volume of liquid feces and as big as my chest. The wall had been stretched tissue paper thin, and was so flimsy I had cut into it without realizing it. The remainder of the autopsy was relatively normal.

I dictated the report, but made no conclusions about the cause of death because I had no way to explain the blood phosphate. Her colon clearly had something to do with it. There is a congenital condition of newborns that causes the colon to dilate and fill with feces, but I'd never heard of such a thing in an adult.

The next day I got a phone call from the Justice of the Peace, who had investigated by visiting her home and talking to her family. She lived in a pig-stye mess with a very unusual twist, her home was filled with hundreds of used Fleet's Phospho-soda enema bottles. Her family said she was obsessed with her bowel movements and gave herself daily enemas.

Bingo!

When I was in medical school we'd learned about obsessive-compulsive behavior, which varied from irritating habits to debilitating compulsions: ritual handwashing dozens of times a day, for example. The conclusion was simple: she was obsessed with her bowel habits and had over-filled her colon with Fleet's phospho-soda, which her blood absorbed with fatal consequences.

I filled out the death certificate this way:

Cause of Death: *Hypocalcemia*

Due to: *Phosphate enema poisoning*

Due to: *Constipation*

Due to:_____

## Afterword

The "Cause of Death" in Texas death certificates is still styled this way. Throughout my career I found it problematical to complete; the bottom line always haunted me. When you start backing down that chain there's really no good place to stop, except with the ultimate entry: "Birth," or should it be "Conception"? Sometimes I was tempted to add a psychiatric entry. "Obsessive-compulsive disorder" seemed to fit in this case.

Readers should not be concerned about giving themselves phosphate poisoning by occasional use of proprietary phosphate enema products. However, somewhat similar cases of low blood calcium due to overzealous use of phosphate enemas in young children.

I reported this case in the Journal of the American Medical Association in 1971. I cannot find another adult case in the medical literature.

\* *In 1970 in Texas there were few cities with formal medical examiner offices. Justices of the Peace held sway over investigations of suspicious or violent deaths and could order an inquest or an autopsy as they saw fit. Getting away with murder, literally, was easier in those days.*

*Dallas County, near to the community where I was working at the time of this case, employed a board certified forensic pathologist, Earl Rose, MD, who also had a law degree. Despite his superb qualifications, his autopsy findings were legally subordinate to those of the JP with jurisdiction, who could rule the manner of death as suicide, for example, even if Earl thought it was murder.*

*Earl was a member of the pathology department at Parkland Hospital, when I was a pathology resident there in the late 1960s.. He was fond of telling us about a ledger he kept locked in his desk drawer. In it he kept notes about cases in which he thought the JP's ruling was wrong. We were forever asking Earl to show it to us, but he never would.*

*Earl also happened to be the pathologist who by law should have autopsied JFK after he died in the Parkland emergency room. Strange as it may seem, Kennedy's assassination was not a federal crime. It was a Dallas County murder. But the Secret Service and FBI took the body over Earl's strenuous and legally correct objection. Military pathologists, who, in my opinion, made a mess of it, did the autopsy in Washington. Not one of them had forensic certification. Conspiracy theories, which I find a waste of time, flourish on this sort of thing.*

*The great irony is this: not only did Dallas have a highly qualified forensic pathologist available to do the Kennedy autopsy, there were superb medical examiner systems in New York, Baltimore, and Richmond, Virginia, each less than an hour's flight away from Washington. Maximum expert help was nearby and was not used. Such a waste.*

CHAPTER 14

# Is Nixon Still President?

**Prologue**

By 1973 I had been nearly eight years without a vacation.  In the military I got thirty days leave each year, but that ended in July 1965.  But through four years of pathology residency and my first four years in practice I never took off more than an occasional long weekend.  Too, I was under a lot of stress.  I had moved to a large Dallas hospital with a group of other pathologists. The situation became unstable and contentious and I found myself in a psychiatrist's office seeking help for depression.  One day we discussed my workaholic lifestyle and it's possible relationship to my mental state.  After an hour of complaining and sighs, my time was up and he walked me to the door.

"Well," I sighed, "I suppose I *should* take a vacation."

"No, Tom," he replied with a mischievous grin, "You *can* take a vacation if you want one."

Seldom has such a simple remark had such a profound effect on me. *Yes!* I thought. *It's true. I am free to take a vacation if I want to.* And with that my wife and I began a life of travel that continues to this day.

Is Nixon still President?" I asked, desperate for news. We were vacationing in a remote part of Jamaica and the guy breakfasting at the next table, a hotel guest we'd not seen before, was reading the New York Times.

He laughed, and thumped the paper for emphasis: "He's still holding on."

This was in the summer of 1974 and Richard Nixon was being hounded to resign as President amid the Watergate scandal. Marianne and I were on a scuba diving vacation in Negril Beach, Jamaica before it became a luxury destination. To our dismay we discovered that our drab little two story hotel offered no TV, newspapers, or room telephone. After a few days I was desperate for something to read other than the book I'd brought, and hoped I could scrounge the Times from the new guest when he finished with it.

We began talking and invited him to join us. As vacationing strangers sometimes do after introductions, we exchanged a few personal details and we learned he was a writer. Having a life-long urge to write but having done little with it but try my hand at a few personal stories like this one, I was intrigued and asked him about his career.

He proved a charming conversationalist and told us his adult life began as a ship's steward—a waiter—in the U. S. Coast Guard. He had wanted some adventure and enlisted over his parents' objections. "All of my brothers and sisters were studying law or medicine, which made me the black sheep of the family," he said with a chuckle, making light of his race.

His career as a writer began in WWII in the South Pacific when a shipmate asked him to write a love letter to his girlfriend. The guy didn't have the writing skills necessary to impress her and wanted a "flowery" love letter that told of his love, of the exotic ports he visited, and the sites he'd seen. Our new friend wrote the letter and in short order other shipmates made similar requests.

He told us he enjoyed writing those letters so much that he tried his hand at fiction and sent some steamy stories to *True Romance* and similar pulp magazines of the era. After many years of rejection slips he sold a story, which was followed by others on a regular basis. His superiors learned of his success and reassigned him as a journalist. After retiring from the Coast Guard he found regular work as a writer. After several years *Playboy Magazine* hired him to do in-depth interviews with notable figures. It was an impressive list: Muhammad Ali, Martin Luther King, Malcolm X, and other notables.

"Have you written any books?" I asked.

"Well," he said, "it doesn't sound like I wrote it, but my first book was *The Autobiography of Malcolm X.* It's based on the interview I did with him."

I'd finished reading it the week before. That I had read it was as improbable as our meeting. A few weeks earlier I had attended a luncheon and the speaker asked if anyone had read *The Autobiography of Malcolm X.* Not one hand was raised in the sizeable, well-educated, all white audience. The speaker admonished us for our narrow reading habits. The remark hit home with me, so I bought a copy and finished it before we left for Jamaica.

It's hard to say who was more delighted with this revelation: him or me. We began discussing race relations in America and after a while he said, "Do you have time to come up to my room? I have something I want to show you."

He had rented two rooms for an extended time, one for an office, the other as a bedroom. In his office were stacks of cardboard boxes stuffed with research papers, and files containing the draft manuscript of a book he was writing.

We sat enthralled as he recounted the story: how he had traced his genealogy back to Africa, to a boy who had been kidnapped in 1767 and brought to Maryland and sold as a slave.

The tale was astounding. I'd been raised with family stories and had a natural interest in family history, but I'd never heard of any black American tracing his genealogy back to slaves brought from Africa. If asked to speculate, I'd have said it was impossible. "Surely," I said, "somebody is interested in publishing this."

He grinned and said, "Yes, I've been negotiating with a publisher, and I think we've got a deal."

Thus began a memorable few days. We shared meals and bought one another drinks at the bar as we talked about everything from Watergate and Richard Nixon, to Malcolm X and Martin Luther King. Seldom have I enjoyed such an extended series of conversations.

In one of those conversations we were interrupted by one of the teenage Jamaican boys who helped on the scuba boat. He was a perfect physical specimen, as only youth can be. Slim, muscled, glistening black skin, and perfect white teeth that gave him a dazzling smile.

After he departed, I said, "I'd like to see the coronary arteries on that boy; I bet they're as big around as your pencil," referring to the one our new friend kept in his shirt pocket.

"Tell me more," he said, pulling the pencil and a notebook from his pocket. As I spoke he scribbled. I explained that the boy looked healthy and fit and surely must eat a healthier diet than the fast food so prevalent in the United States. I couldn't imagine him having any of the coronary artery disease that begins in the crib in the U. S. He encouraged me to say more, and took notes all the while.

Flattered by his interest, I asked him why. "It's just part of my education," he said. "You can't write what you don't know. And when you write, write what you know the best."

## Epilogue

It has taken me 30-plus years to learn that lesson. I've written a couple of medical textbooks, but personal stories like this one are the easiest to do and the most satisfying.

Our new acquaintance's name, Alex Haley, meant nothing to us or to anyone else in America at the time, because his novel would not be published for several more years. It became the blockbuster bestseller "Roots," which spawned a television mini-series and won him a Pulitzer Prize.

I corresponded with Alex for a few years. After he achieved worldwide fame as the author of *Roots* he invited us to spend some time at his home in Jamaica, but we were never able to make it work out. We never met again.

CHAPTER 15

# Something Bit Me

**Prologue**
The unstable situation at the Dallas hospital blew up and in 1976 I moved to a hospital in El Paso. This trip occurred the last week of August 1976.


**The two-lane road snaked smoothly** through the rolling hills of western New Mexico, stands of dark timber separating glades dotted with wild flowers. My little red Porsche, not always smooth or reliable, was humming along perfectly, hugging the curves with confidence. I was on my way from El Paso to the Grand Canyon for a float trip on the Colorado River. Life was good. Lost in the moment, I topped a hill and came face-to-face with a locomotive coming at me down the middle of the road. Or so it seemed. Actually, it was dead still, but it was the genuine article, a hulking black iron relic of bygone industrial might, with no railroad in sight. Seemingly dropped from the heavens, its mighty mass of iron obscured the long, low flatbed trailer beneath it. I stopped to take in the scene as the crew appeared. They were ferrying the engine to a railroad buff's private museum. Mechanical trouble had occurred and the tractor had limped away for repairs, leaving the locomotive sitting in the highway. I had no way of knowing at the instant, but it was the first of a string of unlikely moments destined to confront me in the coming week.

The next morning the twenty rafters in our group were deposited at a riverside shack at Lee's Ferry, an historic river crossing on the Colorado where our raft was nosed into the bank with several others. They were made from big silvery pontoons of the type used by U.S. Army engineers to build floating bridges across European rivers during World War II. To make a raft merely lash five together side by side. The result was an unsinkable, unflippable river Titanic equal to the wildest water the Colorado had to offer.

The focus of the moment, however, was the shack, which housed a store selling beer, soft drinks, snacks, sunscreen and other sundries popular with rafters. Other groups were busy provisioning their rafts, shuttling back and forth lugging sacks of goodies and cases of beer. The crowd was mostly loud, young and male, a considerable contrast to our relatively sedate group that included older adults, children and grandchildren, whose tastes favored soft drinks, chips and candy bars.

Amid shouts and waves the other groups pushed into the current and disappeared downstream around a bend while we were loading up. Our group departed last.

As the trip unfolded we frequently leapfrogged other rafts as they took time out on the bank. Each group took on a certain personality according to the rafters on board. Two rafts stood out, one because of an attractive young woman who wore a very skimpy swimsuit beneath a huge yellow straw hat, and another raft that seemed to have more than its share of boastful, profane young males, most of whom apparently worked together in law enforcement.

The first day proved a template for those that followed: drifting down the mostly placid river and running the occasional rapid interspersed with meals, side trips and overnight camps on the bank.

A few days into the trip we rounded a curve on the river to see two men waving to us from the bank.

Our otherwise unflappable guide exclaimed, "What the hell! There's no trail down here!" He had just explained that the canyon rim was thousands of feet above. Adding to the incongruity, the men were dressed in street clothes—slacks, short-sleeved white dress shirts, blue ties and loafers—and they were waving us down like they were hailing a taxi on a street corner in Manhattan. Like the locomotive, they looked as if they had dropped from the heavens.

We coaxed the raft to the bank and asked what was going on.

"Can you guys tell us where we are?" one of them said. I was tempted to say, You are in the bottom of the Grand Canyon. But I didn't.

They explained that they were helicopter pilots and had landed their chopper just over a nearby ridge. They were ferrying the chopper, a brand new model, to a location where the navigation instruments were to be installed. They had seen us from the air, they were lost, getting low on fuel, and needed directions.

Because I had a private pilot's license I was familiar with the air navigation maps they were carrying. Our guide knew where we were on the river, so we laid out the maps and together pinpointed their location. They thanked us and gingerly picked their way over a small rise and disappeared. In a few minutes we heard the whine of a jet turbine and the whack of rotors. The chopper eased into sight and labored upward. We watched until it disappeared over the rim of the canyon heading in the direction we'd pointed.

We continued on our way and, save for the events of the last full day, time passed pleasantly and uneventfully. The girl in the big straw hat and bikini continued to draw comments from our group as we leapfrogged one another going downstream. On the bank she sat regally apart, her head buried in a book. As they passed us while we were ashore she perched on the pile of duffel bags in the center of the raft. She never rode the nose, a coveted spot for most because it offered the wildest bucking passing through rapids. Also impossible to miss was the raft with the law enforcement brigade, which were boisterously reducing their store of beer.

☆ ☆ ☆

Our final full day on the river brought us to Beaver Creek, which our guide had described on several occasions as being worth the two-hour hike that would take us to Beaver Falls. The long hike discouraged everyone but an athletic young woman, another guy and me. Our guide led the way.

It was easy walking. The trail wasn't steep and most of the time we were in the creek bed, which was shady and surprisingly lush, with wild grapes, cottonwood, beaver dams, and an abundance of other greenery. As we neared Beaver Falls the trail took us out of the creek bed and up the side of the canyon. At the peak of the trail we emerged from the shadows into direct sunlight and paused to enjoy the view. It was spectacular: rank upon rank of cliffs and buttes receding in to the distance. It was a good place for a break. As we sat down the young girl suddenly jumped and said, "Something bit me!" Only then did we hear the buzz of rattles and see that she had, quite literally, sat down on a rattlesnake.  She was wearing a bikini swimsuit with a cotton tee shirt top over it and the snake had bitten her on the buttock where the edge of her swimsuit bottom curved between her legs.  Fortunately, the snake was small, just four rattles, and not big enough to deliver a lethal dose of venom for an adult, but any rattlesnake bite can be very troublesome.

We killed the snake with a rock and I broke off the rattlers to give to her later as a memento.

Ordinarily when I'm traveling I don't tell people I'm a physician.  On the one hand it invites questions and revelations I'd rather not know, and on the other hand it often spurs discussions about health policy, politics, medical practice and so on, which I find tiresome.  But now I had to confess.

What to do?

Standard practice for venomous snakebite to an arm or leg is to use a tourniquet, keep the patient quiet and send for help.  Walking or other activity stimulates circulation, which washes venom out into the blood.  The anatomy of the wound prevented use of a tourniquet to slow blood flow and distribution of the venom.  She faced a two-hour hike to get back to the raft.

Cutting open the bite and sucking out the venom was out of the question, mainly because it was useless.  Anti-venin was the best remedy, but we didn't have any.

The guide and I had a quick discussion and agreed there was no alternative but for her to walk back to the raft where there was an emergency radio. I reassured her that she would be okay because the snake was small. I wasn't entirely confident of this advice, but hope is a valuable resource.

The guide told me privately that the raft had no antivenin because the authorities considered that its use without proper medical supervision could be as dangerous as snakebite itself. Severe, even fatal, allergic reactions could occur.

Amid the confusion, anxiety and discussion, she remained remarkably calm. She was self confident and exceptionally fit and I learned later that she was an Ohio high school state champion track and diving athlete.

The guide and girl turned back down the trail for the main river, and, strange as it seems now, the other guy and I continued up the trail a short way to Beaver Falls. It was fruitless for us to go back with them. I had no medical equipment and the raft's medical kit was useless in this situation. After we made our leap from the top of the falls we started the hike back, hoping to catch up.

We hadn't gone far along the trail when we came upon a group of four guys I recognized from the law enforcement, beer-drinkers raft. One of them was slumped on the trail. I said I was a physician and asked if I could help.  His buddies said he was weak and couldn't walk anymore.  I asked if he was drunk.  They said he wasn't but had been drinking too much for most of the trip and they thought he was dehydrated and tired.  I asked him a few questions, to which he responded listlessly but coherently.  I concluded their assessment was about right.  What he needed was rest and fluids with a bit of salt supplement, but he was a two-hour hike from getting anything but water, so the conversation turned to how to get him back to the river.

Together we hoisted him to his feet.  He was big man and teetered for a moment before plopping down again in the trail, head on his knees.  I implored him to stand up but he shook his head in protest.  Finally, we tried to carry him, one person on each leg and arm and one on his head, but after a few steps it proved impossible to continue.  I was nearly at my wit's end.  Our rafts were waiting and we were already late, and I wanted to get back to the river to check on our snakebite victim.  So I told him an exaggerated version of the danger he was in, hoping to motivate him to walk even though he thought he couldn't.  It had the desired effect.  With the fear of God properly installed, he staggered to his feet, and down the trail we went, each of us taking turns under his arms keeping him propped up.

The shadows were long when we neared the main river and reached a steep, twisty part of the trail.  I worried he might fall and we'd have an even bigger mess. It was at this point that I hatched a plan to float him out to the river. The creek had begun to merge with the side-water of the river and was deep enough to swim. Leaving one guy with the lawman, the rest of hiked down to the river, where I discovered that my raft had departed with the snakebite girl. The beer-drinkers raft was waiting.

Their guide said that our guide and victim had made it back to the river and she seemed to be holding up well. They'd tried the emergency radio, but had no luck. The emergency plan depended on contacting tourist aircraft flying the canyon, but none had responded to the distress calls. The guide then decided to send our raft and patient down to the next campsite. In the meantime he would make a several hour hike to the Havasupai Indian Reservation up a side canyon to call for a helicopter rescue.

We gathered a stack of lifejackets and hiked back to the lawman, strapped them on his chest, arms and legs and heaved him into the creek. I held his head out of the water and the others tugged him along.

By the time all of this was settled and the lawman was lying atop the pile of duffel bags it was dark, but off we went on tense, quiet ride. We bounced from one side of the river to the other and washed through several small rapids, which the guide knew posed no danger. After an hour or so of this we saw lights ahead and nosed our way to shore to join the other rafts beached there.

Then I heard about the helicopter rescue attempt. Our guide had succeeded and the U.S. Army dispatched a helicopter, but the chopper hadn't been able to get the girl because it couldn't find a place to land in the dark. They tried hovering but couldn't get low enough long enough to toss her into the door. Worse, they hadn't left any medical supplies for me. They'd assumed they would be able to load the patient, so hadn't bothered to bring any. They left word they'd be back at first light the next morning at a second site downstream.

I found our snakebite victim huddled with her brothers near our group's campfire. She was in remarkably good shape. Her pulse was slow and steady, she had no respiratory distress, and was emotionally composed. Her buttock was about what I expected, bluish black and very hard. The only thing I had to offer was some antihistamine capsules known for their strong drowsy side effect. She didn't need antihistamine but sleep would be good.

After settling down with a bite to eat, I received a visit from the guide from the raft carrying the girl with the big straw hat. She was having trouble breathing. I found her sitting alone. She was agitated, breathing heavily and complaining of tingling in her face and hands—a classic case of anxiety hyperventilation. I didn't ask her what she was anxious about. It's best to avoid the topic—it takes too long, it's no time for psychotherapy, and most patients can't say why they are anxious. So I spent a few minutes reassuring her she would be okay and gave her an antihistamine tablet. Soon she calmed down and went to sleep.

The next morning the chopper picked up our snakebite victim. It was a thrill to hear it coming through the dawn light. I recognized the distinctive "whoop, whoop" of a Huey, the famed helicopter of the Vietnam War, a sound riveting to those of us who had personal experience with it. I didn't go down to the landing zone, there was no need of it. This time the girl and her brothers hopped aboard without incident.

As I was having breakfast the bikini rafter came up to me, now sedately dressed and poised.

"I'm sorry," she said. "The circumstances didn't allow for a proper introduction. I'm Evelyn."

"That's okay," I said. "I'm Tom. I'm glad to see you're doing better this morning."

"I mean, too, that I'm sorry for the spectacle I made of myself."

"Well, Shakespeare said it best: 'All's well that ends well.'"

"That's not quite true, " she said, "because I'm still stuck in the bottom of the Grand Canyon. I can't wait to get out of here."

"Why is that?" I asked.

"This entire trip has been a misadventure. I really didn't want to come but I made myself do it. It's a women's lib thing. I was trying to prove to myself and to my mother that I'm one of the new breed of independent women. I don't know if I'm one of the new breed or not, but I've learned a valuable lesson."

"What's that?" I asked.

"I'm meeting my mother at a Las Vegas hotel tonight. We're checking into a suite. I'm going to the spa at the first available opportunity and get a massage and a manicure and pedicure. I'm never doing anything like this again."

"Okay," I said. "'To thine own self be true.'"

"That's good advice and I intend to follow it. Thank you again."

With that she drew herself upright, turned on her heel and marched away.

I finished breakfast and was rolling up my gear when the dehydrated lawman appeared. He, too, had recovered and was sheepishly apologetic for having caused so much trouble.

After breakfast we remounted our raft and rode the biggest rapid on the river down to the takeout point where helicopters had been booked to take us out. We ascended at a steep angle, close to the wall of the canyon. I've had many chopper rides and this proved to be one of the best. The other passengers seemed more like they were enjoying a roller coaster. I'd had plenty of chopper rides before, sitting in the door, my feet on the runners, a parachute strapped to my back, eager to jump. I could relax and enjoy the view. It was spectacular—like taking an elevator to heaven.

## Epilogue

The rafting outfitter told me later that the girl with the snakebite spent ten days in a Flagstaff, Arizona hospital and recovered completely. It might not have been such a happy ending if the bite had been on her foot or hand. The tissue around a snakebite swells and the tough fascia covering the arms and hands just beneath the skin doesn't allow much room for swelling. As the tissue swells the limb becomes something like an over-inflated basketball. Pressure becomes so high that it strangles the blood supply and causes gangrene of fingers or toes, which in turn can lead to infection and death.

On the other hand, the buttock allows plenty of room for swelling without such complications, because most of the tissue there is fat and the blood supply is meager. This ensures slow uptake of the toxin and avoids the danger of delivering a quick, big dose of venom to the rest of the body.

I called the U. S. Forest Service and learned that it was the first snakebite to a tourist in the Grand Canyon in sixteen years.

# CHAPTER 16

# Death and the Evening News

**Prologue**

In 1977 I moved back to Dallas and established myself in a non-hospital medical laboratory practice. Don Payne was a classmate and friend in college and medical school.

**D**on Payne hanged himself on an otherwise forgettable August day in 1981. The final tableau fitted his proclivity for theatrics. His wife at the time, Jessica Savitch, a weekend anchorwoman for NBC News, had a front row seat from her car in the driveway of their Washington home as the garage door slowly rose to reveal him hanging from a rafter. It was not lost to anyone who knew them that he was suspended in death by the leash of her big dog, which he detested.

That I choose to write about Don is testimony to the enduring affection with which I remember him despite his many problems and failings. Should these pages fall under the eye of his first wife, Dee, or any of his four fine boys, I hope they will realize that I mean well. My prayer is that one day his boys will come to terms with their father's memory as I have with my father's. Both were charismatic, accomplished, and fatally flawed physicians, who charmed patients with hypnotic power and, in the grip of irresistible passions, poisoned most of their relationships. I have come to realize that my brother, Jim, and I, having made good of our lives, are our father's enduring legacy. And so it is with Don's boys, too.

Don and I became friends as at Rice University. We were not close until my junior year when I decided to forego my senior year and attempt to gain admission to medical school a year early. Don was a year ahead of me and my new plan put us on the same schedule. As luck would have it, both of us wound up in the class of 1962 at The University of Texas Southwestern Medical School in Dallas.

It was natural for us to become anatomy lab partners our freshman year. One of my favorite photos is of us standing over our cadaver in freshman anatomy. Don's smile is typically subdued. It has a cat-that-ate-the-canary quality. Don was forever snatching canaries.

He made friends easily and projected an air of affluence and assurance that smacked vaguely of west

Texas oil money and big city ways. Despite my superior academic record I felt inferior and envied his smooth confidence.

He sailed along smoothly, not bothered by his poor grades, which he dismissed with irreverent humor. By contrast, anything less than an A set me to worrying that it could be some harbinger of a slide into trouble. Don was always telling me to loosen up.

The first hint of trouble occurred in our third year of medical school when Don was required to do remedial work because of poor performance in Internal Medicine, a foundational course that weighed heavily in the faculty's assessment of our status. Don's poor grade sprang not from lack of intellect but from irreverence for established norms. Sometimes it didn't make sense to him to attend this conference or to do that chore. So he didn't.

However, despite his trouble with the faculty, he was affable and popular with other students, which led to his election as our school's representative to the new Student American Medical Association. His duties involved some air travel and long distance phone calls, both of which were expensive and somewhat of a luxury in those days. Another hint of things to come was an investigation into his expense account and making unauthorized calls. It sounded serious to me, but he shrugged it off and somehow it came to nothing. Gulp... another canary.

After graduation we went our separate ways for internship, but kept in touch and planned to reunite in the military after interning for a year. We requested assignment to Washington, DC. Don had some connection—he always did—and wound up with a desk job, no patients to see and an opportunity to hob-nob with military and civilian swells. I was assigned to the Pentagon clinic, a job I quickly came to loathe despite its pivotal role in my military experience. Our time together was memorable for our involvement in the Kennedy funeral, about which I've written elsewhere, and for our socializing with Don and his wife Dee. The latter reinforced my impression that Don had powers that eluded understanding. They lived far better than we did, but how they did it escaped me. Don confidently spoke of important military matters in his administrative job that made my daily drill tending to the aches and pains of soldiers seem dull by comparison.

We went our separate ways after being discharged from the Army. He did Ob-Gyn training in Washington and I came back to Dallas to study pathology. From that point on I knew only that he had finished his training and had established a thriving practice in Washington with Ethyl Kennedy, JFK's sister-in-law, as a patient.

Then one day in about 1979 I picked up the phone to hear his voice. He was calling from his hospital bed saying he had hepatitis and wanted me to look at his liver biopsy slides. This marked the beginning of a series of trips to Dallas to ask my advice about his health, his failing marriage to Dee, and his romance with Jessica Savitch, a strikingly beautiful blonde who was a rising star at NBC TV news.

During his trips to Dallas Don confessed other problems as well. He told me that he regularly smoked marijuana and used other drugs with Jessica. One such episode later ended her career: a confused, slurred appearance on the weeknight national news. On one of his Dallas visits he offered me a marijuana cigarette, but having seen my father's life wrecked by drugs, it was easy to decline. That he had hepatitis also fit the picture. I wondered if he was injecting drugs, too, and had contracted hepatitis by being careless with needles.

More troubling was that during his visits I could easily see that he was manic—unnaturally high in a way that reminded me of the bipolar (manic-depressive) patients I had seen while working as a paid extern at Timberlawn psychiatric hospital the last two years of medical school. I had learned enough in my time there to worry that he might become depressed. To compound matters he was also enmeshed in a dispute with the hospital where he practiced. They were concerned about his sterile technique in the operating room. I noted silently that it was at least another place where he could have contracted hepatitis. He dismissed the medical staff as too uptight and the hospital administration as meddlesome bullies. In short, it was their fault, not his. They were picking on him because he was successful. This, too, had psychiatric implications.  I worried he was paranoid, as some bipo-lar patients are.

He married Jessica in March 1981 and within weeks I was drawn into their difficulties, getting calls from each about the behavior of the other.  The last time Don and I talked was when he called from a psychiatric hospital.  Typically, he minimized the problem— he was okay, the doctors were wrong, and besides, he said with wry humor, it was Jessica who was driving him crazy.  He left the hospital against advice and went back to Washington, where he hanged himself.

I don't recall how I learned he had died, whether it was from Dee, his former wife, or Jessica.  Dee, how-ever, called to ask my help in seeing that his wish to be cremated would be honored.  Jessica opposed it and was being very difficult about the funeral arrange-ments.  I tracked her down in New York and we had an angry discussion in which I made it clear that I would go to any length to enforce his wishes and she should acquiesce.  She did.

I was a pallbearer at the funeral, where once again I had to mediate, this time between Dee and Jessica.  Jessica haughtily informed the priest that she was the widow and Dee was nothing more than an ex-wife and that she, Jessica, was entitled to sit at the front of the church and Dee must sit further back, which sepa-rated Dee from her four grieving sons, who were still youngsters.  I tried to get Jessica to relent, but she was adamant and the service went on with Dee in the back.

Dee accepted this insult with the dignity for which she is widely admired.


## Epilogue

As I write I can see on my desktop a small, stylized brass owl, a reminder of the mascot of Rice University, and a gift from Don on his first visit to Dallas to ask my advice about his hepatitis. He was always thoughtful that way.

Jessica died accidentally in 1983. She, her boy-friend and her dog, the one Don hated, drowned when the car in which they were riding took a wrong turn after dinner and tipped upside down into a canal.

Don's ashes rest in a small outdoor columbarium at St. John's Episcopal Church on Lafayette Square across from the White House. Prior to his burial I knew nothing of columbaria. My only knowledge of cremation came from occasional newspaper articles about survivors scattering ashes in some special place. That there was an alternative to burial in a commercial cemetery was a revelation, and it was the perfect answer to a festering problem that had been with me since the death of my father: how to escape the distasteful practices of the funeral industry.

When I was in active practice as a pathologist I did occasional private autopsies, most of which occurred in funeral homes where I got an insider's view of practices that regularly refreshed the painful memory of my father's funeral when I was nineteen.

As the older child it fell to me to go with Mother to make the arrangements. Black-clad attendants ushered us through the ritual, the sales opportunity poorly concealed by feigned somber. My father had made it known that he wanted his funeral to be "in keeping with my modest station in life," but we were shamelessly pressed at every turn to do something more than what my mother knew he had in mind. It left a mark.

# CHAPTER 17

# Surviving Doctor Korzhescu

**Prologue**

My laboratory practice in Dallas flourished. One of the services we offered was as laboratory consultants and off site laboratory directors for small suburban and rural hospitals, a need that developed in the wake of the coming of Medicare in 1965. Among other effects, the flood of Medicare money stimulated the construction of shiny new hospitals in rural towns, most them more a testimony to vanity than need. Keeping the beds full required doctors, but manpower lagged, especially in windswept reaches of west Texas. Desperate to attract new doctors, some became uncritical judges of the few applicants they found.

Regulations required that every hospital retain a pathologist. Our job was to make monthly visits to inspect the hospital laboratory and check quality control documents. In return the hospital and doctors sent us their biopsies and surgery specimens, for which we billed. New doctor names appeared and just as regularly disappeared on the paperwork submitted with the specimens.

I sat at a large table doing "the gross," a term for the naked eye description of the size, shape and other details of specimens submitted by surgeons or other doctors for pathologic examination and diagnosis. Good practice demanded that virtually anything removed from a patient be submitted, even if only for documentation that, in fact, something was removed. Foreign objects, for example, may be submitted for exactly that reason—I once described a peanut removed from the airway of a child. My practice mainly served doctor's offices, which submitted skin, prostate and other small biopsy specimens. But because I consulted with a few small hospitals in west Texas, I occasionally received larger specimens: breasts, stomachs, gallbladders, appendices, and so on.

At my left elbow was one end of a long rank of mostly small glass jars, each containing a specimen submerged in formaldehyde preservative. My job was to examine each specimen, dictate an eyeball description and submit a thin slice or two for microscopic study.

The next specimen was a fist-size lump of fat in a quart jar. The paperwork accompanying the specimen indicated the patient was a 12 year-old boy with a fatty tumor of the groin. Nothing unusual there—fatty tumors (lipomas) are innocuous. And they are common—most of them grow just beneath the skin and are removed for cosmetic purposes.

Holding the specimen with long forceps and twisting it this way and that to measure it with a small ruler, for the zillionth time I said something like, "Okay, the next specimen is number 2915, Jesus Hernandez. The specimen is a smooth, ovoid, yellow, fatty mass about nine by five by five centimeters."

I sliced the specimen in half to inspect the interior. Sure enough, most of it was uniform, smooth, yellow fat, but in the middle was ... well, I didn't know what it was. It was round, about half an inch in diameter, and had an internal anatomy of its own. It was firm, with a rather thick wall and a mostly hollow center. Was it a worm? A congenital abnormality? The latter popped to mind because tissues in the developing fetus undergo amazing contortions, move from one place to another, and sometimes leave behind little remnants of normal tissue in odd places, which are not discovered until years later, if ever.

I made a series of bread-loaf cuts, which revealed the thing to be a tube about three inches long running down the center of the fat that made up the remainder of the specimen. I sat, staring—lipomas just don't have this sort of thing inside.

I'd never seen anything even remotely like it. I looked at the paperwork again, grasping for a clue. The boy's name was Hispanic, and the specimen had been removed at a small hospital in far West Texas by a doctor with an Eastern European name, and a poor grasp of English. He hadn't been in town long and I'd met him once on one of my consultation visits to the hospital's tiny lab. Maybe the boy emigrated from South or Central America, lots of worm infestations down there. But worms belong in the intestines, the heart, the liver, even the brain. But fat? I'd never heard of it.

"What's the matter Doctor McConnell," the tissue tech asked, alerted by my vacant stare. "I don't know," I said, and continued looking at the strange thing, hoping that if I looked long enough a snap of recognition would occur. It didn't. I finally gave up, consoled with the knowledge that if you practice pathology long enough you'll see one of everything.

I continued describing the specimen. "In the center of the specimen is a firm, tan, discrete object, about ten to twelve millimeters in diameter and about seven to eight centimeters long, which extends to one end of the specimen. Representative slices are submitted for microscopic examination."

I sliced thin pieces from the ends and middle of the strange thing and slid them over to the tissue tech. She put them in small, perforated metal containers

for the elaborate overnight processing that would ultimately yield microscopic slides.

The next morning I'd forgotten about the case
when a technician delivered several big white trays
lined with neat rows of shiny glass slides, each holding
a bright red and blue-stained slice of tissue. I flipped
the switches to turn on my microscope and the dictat-
ing apparatus, and began the daily surgical pathology
drill—slap a slide on the microscope platform, look
at it for a while, decide what was going down there
among the cells and dictate a "micro," a description of
the microscopic findings that would be wedded to the
"gross." At the bottom of such reports is the diagnosis.
For example, "Prostate biopsy: No evidence of malignancy," and so on. Most cases are straightforward; the
diagnosis is clear in an instant. If it wasn't clear, my
habit was to set it aside and go to the next easy case in
order to get the workload out. Difficult cases required
further study, reading, or consultation with a colleague.

"All right, the next case is 2915. Microscopic study
reveals . . . " I stopped, transfixed: staring back at me
from the slide was a normal appendix. I can count on
the fingers of one hand the times I've been surprised
by microscopic findings so completely unexpected—
one other is a breast cancer I saw in a male who came
to the ER for a lump in his breast.

How in God's name to explain such a thing. The
appendix is in the abdomen, not in the groin. Maybe
the wrong paperwork was submitted and this was Jane

Doe's appendix and Jesus Hernandez' lipoma was somewhere else with Jane Doe's paperwork.

I called the tissue lab and asked them to scan our records for another specimen from the hospital involved. Nope. This was the only specimen from them in the last few weeks. "They don't do much surgery out there, Dr. McConnell," the supervisor reminded me. It was true. The hospital was in a remote small town that was desperate to lure doctors to keep its doors open. Physicians came and went, some of whom, as I was beginning to learn, were foreign medical graduates with marginal training and shady pasts.

Then it hit me. This was a hernia of the femoral canal and the idiot surgeon didn't recognize it. A hernia is a protrusion of tissue that works its way through a weak spot or opening into a place it doesn't belong. In this instance the appendix—with a substantial cloak of fat—had slid down beside the femoral artery, the main artery to the leg. Where the femoral artery leaves the abdomen and enters the leg is a well-known weak spot through which loops of intestine can stray into the upper thigh. So what, you might say. But remember, the appendix is attached to the large intestine, which meant the part of the intestine was down in the thigh, too.

The boy must have had a bulge in his groin. The doctor saw that it was immediately beneath the skin, just like a lipoma should be, and it was soft but resilient, just like a lipoma should be. The boy's mother was worried. What to do? The surgeon did what surgeons do, he cut it out.

But, so what? This is what. In removing the mass he cut across the base of the appendix where it joins the large bowel. In and of itself this is not bad, that's how appendectomies are done every day. The problem is this—after amputating the appendix he didn't stitch closed the hole in the bowel because he didn't know what he'd done. The appendix contains feces. I was certain the boy was going to develop a severe abdominal infection—if he didn't already have one—caused by bacteria leaking from his intestine.

I buzzed the receptionist and asked her to get the doctor on the phone. In a few minutes she had him on the line. The conversation went something like this.

"Hello, Doctor Korzhescu,* this is Doctor McConnell from Dallas, your pathology consultant. I'm calling about the specimen you sent us on Jesus Hernandez."

"Oh, yes," he said cheerily. "Very nice. A good boy."

"That mass you removed from his groin."

"Yes. Yes."

"Well, it turns out to be a femoral hernia that had the appendix in it."

"Yes. The lipoma?" He portrayed no surprise.

Trying to give him the benefit of doubt, I said, "It's not a lipoma. It's the appendix and some fat. Did you stitch the bowel closed after your appendectomy?"

"No appendectomy. A lipoma. Thank you. No worry. A strong boy. Very fine. Very fine. "

I was getting nowhere. By the time we parted I thought I'd heard him tell me the boy had spent one night in the hospital and had already been sent home. Rather than try to deal further with the doctor, I called the hospital administrator, a sensible woman I had come to admire in the course of my periodic visits. I explained the problem to her and she said she would inquire of the nurses and the town's other doctor, a semi-retired general practitioner who had originally seen Jesus. She called back that afternoon to tell me that Jesus was at home and no one had heard of any problems.

On my next consultation visit to the hospital a month later Dr. Korzhescu was gone. On the advice of the hospital's lawyer the hospital administrator wouldn't tell me anything more. Jesus had recovered completely.

## Epilogue

Those days are gone. Almost all of these small town hospitals no longer function as such. Some remain as doc-in-a-box urgent care facilities. Many of these have no doctor—nurses or certified physician assistants provide the front line care now. Others serve as nursing homes and some simply sit empty, relics of once-upon-a-time.

*Not his real name.*

CHAPTER 18

# Leaving Cancer Alone

**Prologue**
Another episode from my years in independent laboratory practice.

I fished the little piece of tissue from its container. It was just another small biopsy, firm and gray from an overnight soaking in formaldehyde. On the accompanying paperwork I could see that the patient was a 69 year-old man. In the "Specimen" box the surgeon had written "Thigh mass." I dictated a short description and sliced a thin sample from the middle. Giving it no more thought, I passed the sliver of tissue across to a technician who would shepherd it through the overnight ritual that would turn it into a microscopic slide.

The next day I plowed through the trays of slides, each of which offered the usual array of common diagnoses: skin warts and other innocuous lumps and bumps that are the daily diet of pathologists examining outpatient biopsies. More or less on autopilot, I slid the next slide under the scope. I saw a sea of bizarre cells with microscopic features so wild that there could be no doubt that it was a vicious malignancy. The only thing remaining was to decide exactly what kind.

I walked the slide around to other pathologists. All agreed with my provisional diagnosis: a well known but rare tumor that usually occurs in bones or the soft tissues of the body.

I called the surgeon with the grim news. He told me the tumor was deep in the thigh and perilously close to the big nerves and blood vessels that supply the lower limb. I promised to send it to a consultant pathologist for a second opinion because the implications were so dire. There was no way to cut it out and spare the limb. Amputation was the only choice. The standard therapy was radical, disarticulation through the hip joint with removal of the buttock and entire leg. Surgery, though crippling, offered a reasonable chance for longer life.

Weeks passed without further thought of the matter until I got a message from an internist asking me to look again at the case and give him a call. It seemed odd. Internists usually don't insert themselves into cases like this. Surgeons and cancer specialists, yes; but internists, no.

The internist in question was one I knew because he marched to the tune of a different drummer. Famously iconoclastic, he was forever questioning the received wisdom of the general medical community, even about firmly established notions. He practiced in a small office with only one employee, and he often answered his own office phone.

When I called he came on the line instantly. He asked a few questions about the case and then invited me to his office to discuss it with him, explaining that he was the patient's primary physician and had originally discovered the lump. We arranged a time to visit, and I hung up more puzzled than before. What further could he have to do with this case other than offering general care after the surgeons finished their grim chore?

As we talked about the case I found he'd done his homework. He was very knowledgeable about his patient's cancer and about the patient, having made a house call to study how the patient lived and how he might get around without his leg. We talked about the patient at length. After a while he paused, deep in thought. Then he said something like this, "What would you say, Tom, if I told you I was thinking about recommending to this patient that we leave this thing alone, that we not cut off his leg, and that he not have chemotherapy?"

I asked him to explain. "Well," he said, "you know what they're going to do. They're going to take his leg off at the hip.  This guy will be 70 next year, he still has sex with his wife, he plays a little golf, he goes to the market.  In short, he has a life, all of which will come to a miserable end if we go forward with what the experts say.  He'll be in a wheel chair.  Sex, golf and freedom to get around will come to an end. "So," he continued, "I'm serious when I ask: 'Do you think I'm out of my mind?'"

Now I could see where he was going.  He really did want to know if I thought his idea was so far off base that I might, for example, testify against him if it came to a malpractice trial or a disciplinary hearing.

As we continued to talk the wisdom of his idea became more evident.  "No," I finally said, "I don't think you're nutty.  In fact, the more I think about this case the more sense you seem to make."

That is what he recommended, and the patient took his advice.  Years later I asked the internist about it.  The tumor, which was fist-size when diagnosed, had grown slowly.  It did not spread to other parts of the body, nor had it much interfered with the patient's life until he was several years older, at which time it had grown to football size and interfered with the motion of his leg to such a degree that he had to give up golf and was confined to a wheel chair.  Eventually the tumor became massive and proved fatal.

Looking back, the patient's doctor was unusually wise … and brave.  It was a good decision, made by the type of physician everyone should have.

CHAPTER 19

# How Much Is Them Fries?

**Prologue**
Near my office in the mid-1980s.

My office was near a fast food restaurant where I sometimes went for lunch. It featured a small outdoor dining area near the street, and when the weather was right it was a good place to sit, watch the people go by, and feed bits of french fries to the ever-present flock of sparrows.

On a sunny, unusually warm day just before Christmas I took a late lunch and ordered a burger, fries and soft drink. The outside tables were empty, so I chose one in the sun and laid out the Wall Street Journal to enjoy my break. I was absent-mindedly tossing bits of french fries to the sparrows when I noticed a boy had materialized at the next table.

He was grade-school age and thin, with large eyes, shabby clothes and a direct gaze.

"How much is them fries?" he asked.

"Would you like some?" I said.

He came over wordlessly and sat next to me on the bench. I pushed the fries over to him. He hesitated, took one, pinched off a piece and tossed it to the birds. As they fluttered over their bounty, he looked at the fry in his hand, then at me.

"It's okay," I said.

He downed the fry and said, "Them 's sure good, mister."

"Here," I said, giving him a five dollar bill, "get something to eat."

Shortly he came back with a burger, fries and a big soda. He dutifully placed the change in front of me and spread his meal beside mine. As he ate we talked. I asked about school, home and family. His replies, as direct as his gaze, were a tale impossible odds—poverty, neglect, a broken family.

He ate slowly, careful to toss a piece of each fry to the birds. When I finished my meal, he stopped eating, too.

"I have to go now," he said, wrapping the remaining half of the burger and fries in a napkin. He stuffed them back into the sack, obviously saving something for later.

He said, "Thank you, mister."

I offered him my hand. We shook and he walked away. As he neared the sidewalk he turned and waved. He took a few more steps, turned again and held up the sack. "These is for my friend. He's your color, you know." And then he was gone.

## Epilogue

Afterward I went inside and asked the manager and employees if they'd seen him before or knew anything about him. No. They couldn't remember him being in the store before. I went back for lunch every day that week, hoping to find him, but to no avail. Over the next few years I regularly ate lunch there hoping we could reconnect. I never saw him again.

# CHAPTER 20

# Forget It

**Prologue**

These episodes span the arc of my career from medical student to practicing physician. None of them had anything to do with the practice of pathology.

The internal medicine resident gave me a long stare and said, "*Doctor* McConnell," with sarcastic emphasis to remind me that I was still a junior medical student, "if you expect gratitude, forget it."

I was working on a chart in a nurse's station with several other junior students. Novitiates all, we were learning the drill. Keeping the chart up to date was a religious obligation. Ours was an irreverent mantra: "The patient died but the chart was well." Most of our jottings were simple stuff: physical exam findings and progress notes, periodic observations about new patient developments. We even got to write a few orders, mainly for the routine stuff, baths, enemas, diet and so on.

After making a long note about a particularly difficult patient, I spouted off to no one in particular how ungrateful she and her husband were for my ministrations. A resident nearby overheard me and set me straight.

It was a rude introduction to reality, which shattered the glossy image I had of healing the sick and helping the poor on the floors of Parkland Hospital in 1961. I had spent more than a week hovering over a borderline retarded young woman with a strange feverish illness. Frustratingly, her diagnosis was elusive and she was thoroughly dislikable: disruptive, demanding, and crude. My job was to draw blood, start IVs, collect urine and stool specimens, and tend to the dozens of other menial tasks allotted to junior medical students.

Her husband was equally troublesome. He was unkempt, obstreperous, and more interested in having sex with her in a four-bed ward than in her health. To top it off they checked out of the hospital against medical advice while loudly complaining that we hadn't figured out what was wrong with her, that the food was lousy, and they would be better off at home, all of which was arguably true. To me it was good riddance. As I watched them shuffle past the nurse's station on the way out, I complained and got a jolt in return—a short lecture on the ethic of medical care: you do the right thing because it's right, not because you expect a reward like a treat tossed to a dog that does a trick. And you owe the same compassion and scientific duty to every patient, even if they are demanding, ungrateful, smelly jerks.

✼ ✼ ✼

In the 1970s I was reminded again. My wife and I were having dinner in a small restaurant at a low-budget ski resort in northern New Mexico. Seated at the next table was a boisterous group of eight men, apparently several generations of a family enjoying dinner after a day of elk hunting. Steaks and beer were the order of the evening, and all of them were drunk. Their slurred banter and loud laughter made our dinner less than pleasant.

Suddenly the laughter stopped and chairs scraped about. My back was turned but the look on my wife's face told me something unusual was up. I turned to see that the oldest of the group, a grandfatherly sort seated at the head of the table, had fallen over into his plate. Most of the others stared with bovine indifference, but one of the younger ones was out of his chair, lurching toward the fallen patriarch.

I jumped up to see if I could help. My first thought was that he was having an epileptic seizure, but a few seconds of observation made that an unlikely possibility: no trembling or thrashing about. He was still as death. I asked if he was diabetic and in the melee of answers I didn't hear anyone say Yes, and quickly dismissed the idea because coma doesn't occur so quickly. Did he have heart disease, I shouted. Not that anyone knew. Does he take any medicines? No one seemed to know. Finally, I wondered if he was just dead drunk, but alcoholic coma doesn't occur so abruptly either.

I grabbed him by the collar and pulled his head out of the plate, tilting his head backward so I could see his face and eyes. After clearing away the mashed potatoes and steak sauce, I spread his eyelids. His eyes were rolled back but I could see that his pupils still reacted to light. At least his brainstem was alive. By now his face had turned dusky blue and it finally dawned on me that he might have choked on his food. The syndrome is classic: older people, often with dentures, frequently intoxicated, poorly chewed steak a common culprit—a partially chewed piece moves too far back on a wobbly, intoxicated tongue and reaches the point of reflex swallowing, which no amount of concentration can reverse. The piece is too big to go down and lodges deep in the throat, blocking the airway and preventing speech—part of the syndrome is the silence of the victim. This guy had collapsed without a word as far as I could tell.

Grabbing his hair with one hand and his chin with the other, I pried his mouth open and peered in to find loose dentures and a slimy mess of partially chewed food. But no steak. Compounding the problem, his tongue fell back into his throat, blocking my view. Thinking that I might be able to dig out something deeper, I stuck my hand as far as possible into the hole, but couldn't feel anything; and he didn't gag, which confirmed how far gone he was.

It was time to try the Heimlich maneuver, a procedure designed to dislodge objects lodged in the throat and block the airway. It is now widely taught but was a new concept at the time. I tilted him back so that his head lolled over the back of the chair, grateful that is was a small chair that I could reach around. I squatted, reached around him and the chair and joined my hands at the lower end of his chest. I gave a heave, digging my clasped hands into the lower end of his breastbone, trying to propel air out of the lungs with enough force to pop out the obstructing mass, if one was there. With this he fell forward into his plate again, but nothing came out of his mouth. I jerked him back upright again, and applied a second prodigious jerk, this time not caring if I broke ribs or did other damage. He catapulted forward a second time and a big piece of steak plopped onto his plate as if returning to its rightful place in the universe. He took a huge breath, and then another, and began to stir. Meanwhile, we stared as if watching the awakening of a sleeping beast. Soon he roused enough to sit upright on his own and offered me a quizzical look. He had no idea what had happened.  The two guys who had gotten up sat back down.  I excused myself to wash my hands and returned to finish dinner.  They partied on, albeit less loudly.  I was certain they did not understand what happened.  We finished our meal and left without so much as a nod from the men at the table.

✵ ✵ ✵

Another episode occurred in the 1990s on a cruise down the Italian coast.  While traveling I rarely reveal that I am a physician because it tends to direct conversation toward medical subjects, and because it sometimes leads to requests for opinions or treatment I'd rather avoid.  Most cruise ships have a doctor on board, but this time we were on a ship with a capacity of about 100 passengers, too small for a ship's doctor.

We had just returned to the ship from an afternoon shore excursion when the Captain's voice boomed over the ship's intercom: "Any available physician please call the bridge."  I called, expecting to be one of several on board.  I proved to be the only one.  The Captain gave me a stateroom number and asked that I meet him there to examine a woman.  "We can't wake her up," he said.

I found the Captain and First Officer in the room with two elderly women, both of whom I recognized from the dining room.  One stood nervously by the captain, the other lay abed, apparently asleep.

"I just got back from an all day tour and she's still asleep," the woman said. "Her things are where she left them when we went to bed last night. When I got up this morning she stayed in bed. I imagined she was tired and wanted to skip our outing, so I didn't wake her. When I got back a few minutes ago I found her just like I left her. She hasn't moved an inch."

I pulled back the bedcovers and did a quick assessment. She was wringing wet and her breathing had a forced, mechanical quality. The movements of her chest were not the placid excursions of someone asleep, and she could not be roused, even to a knuckle dug deep into her upper breastbone.

She was deeply comatose. But why? I told the Captain to summon an ambulance and asked her roommate if our patient was diabetic. She was not. I asked for a list of medicines she was taking. Three stood out: two for irregular heartbeat, and Coumadin, a widely prescribed blood thinner. A picture was beginning to form. This combination of drugs is often prescribed together in patients with a certain type of irregular heart rhythm commonly found in older persons. I asked if she had fallen recently. Sure enough, while going up the stairs to dinner the night before she had slipped and banged her head against the handrail. She suffered no apparent injury and continued on to dinner.

That was enough. I told the Captain I was reasonably sure she had a brain hemorrhage. I concluded she had a variety of slow bleeding that occurs over the surface of the brain. This type of bleeding is a hazard with minor head injury in patients taking blood thinners. For certain anatomic reasons the blood accumulates slowly and doesn't produce the dramatic, sudden symptoms of stroke. As blood accumulates it presses on vital parts of the brain and symptoms appear. In this instance the patient became comatose while asleep.

An ambulance arrived and she was whisked away to a hospital. The ship continued on its way, and we finished the cruise uneventfully. After returning to the U. S., I called the cruise line and asked what became of the patient. She had the bleeding I suspected, which was successfully halted and drained by an Italian neurosurgeon. She had returned safely to the U. S. after a week in an Italian hospital.

And one more thing: nowhere along the way did anyone say "Thank you."

## Epilogue

Each of these episodes reveals a failing: my expectation of gratitude. I was raised to count my blessings and be thankful for them. So I expected as much from others. With experience, however, I have gained perspective.

It came from a person important in my career, not a family member, who treated me with unusual generosity over the course of many years. I remain greatly indebted to him.  But I learned that it was his unconscious method of control.  In effect, he bought compliance.  In time, despite his good heart, it bred resentment. A gift ceases to be a gift and becomes a transaction if something is expected in return, even something so insubstantial as gratitude.  It is good manners to say "Thank you," but once is enough.

# CHAPTER 21

# President Ford and the Case of the Missing Adrenal Glands

As I watched **President Gerald Ford's** funeral in January 2007, I fell to thinking of a brief interaction I had with him when he was a Republican Congressman from Michigan. This was before he became Richard Nixon's Vice President and before he became President in the wake of Nixon's resignation after the Watergate scandal. I had written him about the Kennedy autopsy. His response validates history's judgment that Mr. Ford was a decent man with an uncommon common touch.

In the aftermath of the Kennedy assassination Lyndon Johnson appointed a commission to investigate the matter. It included distinguished politicians and public figures, and became known as the Warren Commission after its chairman, Chief Justice Earl Warren. Mr. Ford, a congressman from Michigan, was appointed to it as the senior Republican.

History and events had conspired to make me unusually interested in the Kennedy autopsy. Kennedy was assassinated in Dallas, my hometown; I had grown up shooting high-powered rifles similar to the one used to assassinate Kennedy, and in the few months before he was killed I had been within a few yards of him on several occasions during my duties as a medical officer in the Pentagon. Plus there were the three memorable days I spent involved in the Kennedy funeral.

After the assassination I remained in the Army another nineteen months finishing my active duty obligation. All the while I heard rumors from friends at Parkland Hospital, where I had been as a medical student and where Kennedy had been taken after the shooting. The most interesting of many stories concerned a friend, Jim Carrico, who was a surgery resident at the time of the assassination and later became Chairman of the Department of Surgery. Jim was the first physician to see Kennedy when he arrived in the Parkland emergency room, and the story had it that the White House physician accompanying Kennedy thrust into Jim's hand a syringe of injectable hydrocortisone. This struck me as very unusual because if true it seemed to signal that it was a personal medication and not the type of thing that would have become instantly available in the few minutes it took to arrive at Parkland after the gunshots. I could imagine it being in an emergency kit, but not syringe-ready instantaneously. The list of things that call for regular administration of hydrocortisone is very short and at the top is failure of the adrenal glands, which are the body's natural source. Without hydrocortisone, life is impossible to sustain for more than a few days. This fit with rumors circulating that Kennedy had Addison's disease, a failure of the adrenal glands.

After finishing my stint on active duty I returned to Parkland for specialty training in pathology. It was a good place to get inside information about the assassination, since most of those who had ministered to the dying President were still there. As a pathology resident I did dozens of autopsies in the first couple of years and knew enough to know that Addison's disease is invariably caused by destruction of the glands, an easy thing to document at autopsy.

So, I asked a lot of questions and studied newspaper and medical journal reports that speculated on the matter. Soon things began to add up. I had seen Kennedy at a distance of no more than twenty yards at the Tomb of the Unknown Soldier in Arlington National Cemetery on Veteran's Day 1963, twelve days before he was killed. He looked fit, relaxed and tan, too tan on later reflection. It is a characteristic of Addison's disease for patients to have abnormally dark skin and Kennedy's tan had a bronzed appearance without the ruddiness that comes with sun exposure.

I ordered a copy of the Warren Commission Report and became one of a legion that pored over it, most of them conspiracy theorists interested in the gunshot wounds. My interest, however, was the Kennedy autopsy report and his adrenal glands. My suspicions were confirmed when the autopsy made no mention of the adrenal glands, an omission inconceivable in an ordinary autopsy, much less one on an assassinated president.

I wrote every member of the Warren Commission and to Teddy, Bobby and Jackie Kennedy. I argued that it was a disservice to the nation and to anyone else with a lifelong illness, such as diabetes, for the public not to know that someone so afflicted could serve ably as President.

From each of the Kennedy's I got glossy black and white photographs with public relations form letters. From the members of the Warren Commission I heard nothing … with the singular exception of Gerald Ford, who wrote me a personal letter. Regrettably, I no longer can find it, but I recall it well. It was signed in his distinctive hand, which I came to recognize after he became President, and was typed on fine official congressional stationery. It briefly and pointedly addressed my concerns in a way that made clear this was no pro-forma response. I cannot recall the exact wording, but the essence of the message was that the records were to be sealed for many years and that all of the information that could be released had been included in the public version of the Warren

Commission Report.  It was easy to read between the lines that there was other information that was not to be made public for a long time.

It is now settled history that Kennedy had Addison's disease.  Among the most important supporting documents are the medical records from his back surgery in the 1950s, which discusses the threat Addison's poses for any person having a spinal fusion.  Kennedy was hospitalized under a pseudonym and his case was the subject of an article in a surgery journal.  He is now regarded as the first documented case of a patient with Addison's disease to survive major surgery.

## Epilogue

During the presidential campaign of 1960 against Richard Nixon, Kennedy had been pointedly asked if he had Addison's disease.  He denied so, presumably relying on the original, and long abandoned, definition of Addison's disease: adrenal failure due to adrenal tuberculosis (the original report to the South London Medical Society by Dr. Addison in 1849 described a group of patients with adrenal failure due to tuberculosis of the adrenal glands). Since the advent of the antibiotic era in WWII, tuberculosis has become a very rare cause of Addison's disease.  It is not recorded if anyone ever asked Kennedy if he had "adrenal failure."  To deny when questioned in this manner would have been an outright lie.

# About Author

Thomas H. McConnell, III was born at "old" Parkland Hospital in Dallas in 1937. His initial education was in rural East Texas, in the public schools of Sulphur Springs. He received his undergraduate education at Rice University and his M.D. degree from the University of Texas Southwestern Medical School in 1962. In 1962-63 he was an intern at the University of Mississippi Hospital in Jackson. From 1963-65 he served as a Medical Officer in the U. S. Army, first as a General Medical Officer in the Pentagon and later as Battalion Surgeon with the 101st Airborne Division. He returned to Dallas in 1965 for training in pathology at the "new" Parkland Hospital and UT Southwestern. He was a private practitioner and laboratory entrepreneur from 1969-1991. In 1997 he accepted a teaching appointment in the pathology department at UT

Southwestern, where he remains on the faculty. He is author of *The Nature of Disease* (2007), a textbook of pathology, and is co-author with Kerry Hull of *Human Form, Human Function* (2010), a textbook of anatomy and physiology. He lives in Dallas with Marianne, his wife of 48 years, and two West Highland White Terriers.

# Index

Made in the USA
Las Vegas, NV
06 June 2021